A *few* Words on

YOUR
IDENTITY
IN CHRIST

A 125 Day Discovery of Your Truest Self

Quantity order requests can be emailed to: thefewwomen@gmail.com

A FEW Words on Your Identity in Christ
Publishing Coordinator and Story Collector: Kimberly Joy Krueger

Volume 3 of the "A FEW Words" Devotional Series from FEW International Publications and FEW International Organization, LLC

Contributing Authors: Amy Oaks, Eleanor Weldie, Heather Taylor, Heidi Sampson, Joni Jones, Kimberly Krueger, Lisa Danegelis, Luanne Nelson, Marlene Dawson, Michelle Meade, Nilda Campuzano, Noreen Lessmann, Sue Sherstad, Susan Brozek, Susan Tyler, Tierney Gill, and Traci Weldie

Expert Contributor: Susan C. Brozek, M.S.W., L.C.S.W.

Contributing Editors: Traci Weldie and Kimberly Krueger
Contributing Editor: Eleanor Weldie

Cover Artists: Maci Hahn and Lexi Niedfeldt
Cover Designer: Trace Chiodo; Chiodo Design, chiododesignstudio.com

Interior Layout Designer: Emmie Nosek

Bible verses are taken from biblegateway.com ©1995-2017, The Zondervan Corporation. All Rights Reserved.

ISBN-13: 978-1-949494-08-2

Categories:
Religion & Spirituality/Christian Books & Bibles/Literature & Fiction/Collections & Anthologies
Religion & Spirituality/Christian Books & Bibles/Christian Living/Devotionals
Religion & Spirituality/Christian Books & Bibles/Christian Living/Women's Issues

FEW International Publications
An Extraordinary Publishing Experience

FEW International Publications is a #1 Bestselling Publisher for women authors at all levels who are seeking more from telling their stories than just a printed project. We are privileged to watch FEW Authors connect, learn, grow, and heal through the creation of a written work that impacts others and glorifies God. Find FEW's books at thefewwomen.com and on amazon.com.

Extraordinary Women; Extraordinary Stories
thefewwomen.com

I have no greater joy than to hear that my children are walking in the truth.
3 John 4

After working with women on their spiritual development for decades now, I knew these words penned by John, the Apostle, were the perfect theme for this devotional.

I have seen firsthand, time and again, what happens when a Christian woman walks in the truth of who she is; it always brings pure joy! *I have also seen what happens when she doesn't.*

I believe the importance of walking in the truth of who God is, and equally paramount, *who He says we are,* cannot be overstated. They are both the worthiest pursuits for women who want to experience the abundant life Jesus died to give us. The revelation and implementation of these will, in every case, make a woman unstoppable. Knowing our Father's heart for us and choosing to come into agreement with what He says about us will do nothing short of perfectly position us for our destinies!

And our enemy knows that.

It is my prayer for each woman who reads this book, that she remembers there is a battle for her identity—and her destiny is what is truly at stake. This battle is not against people, it is a spiritual battle won with the Sword of the Spirit, which is the Word of God. It is won by choosing time and again to believe and declare,

What God says about me, is the truest thing about me.

Empowered by the Father's Love, may you choose to agree with and walk in your Identity in Christ!

In His Truth,

Kimberly Krueger
Founder of FEW International Organization, LLC

Table of Contents

God Never Forgets   Marlene Dawson   *Exodus 2:24*   16

God's Love Directs Us to Him   Marlene Dawson   *Exodus 23:20*   18

Abba's Heart   Michelle Meade   *Deuteronomy 1:30-32*   20

Victory in the Battle   Lisa Danegelis   *Deuteronomy 20:4*   22

Sweet Dreams   Heather Taylor   *Deuteronomy 31:8*   24

Watch Your Six!   Nilda Campuzano   *1 Chronicles 16:11-13* 26

The Golden Scepter   Kimberly Krueger   *Esther 5:2-3*   28

Full of Doubt   Heidi Sampson   *Job 13:15a*   30

Safe and Secure in My Savior's Shadow   Tierney Gill   *Psalm 4:8*   32

Don't Talk About My Daughter Like That!   Kimberly Krueger   *Psalm 18:1-2*   34

He Leads in Paths of Righteousness   Sue Sherstad   *Psalm 23:2-3*   36

Taste and See   Michelle Meade   *Psalm 34:8*   38

Beautifully Broken   Tierney Gill   *Psalm 34:17-19*   40

He Inclined to Me   Sue Sherstad   *Psalm 40:1-2*   42

Winding Roads   Sue Sherstad   *Psalm 68:5-6*   44

At My Lowest   Heidi Sampson   *Psalm 103:8*   46

Under Construction   Nilda Campuzano   *Psalm 127:1*   48

I Am Content   Michelle Meade   *Psalm 131:1-2*   50

No More Hiding   Eleanor Weldie   *Psalm 139:1*   52

Mistake or Masterpiece?   Amy Oaks   *Psalm 139:13-14*   54

Healed Brokenness Joni Jones   *Psalm 147:3*   56

What If Tierney Gill   *Proverbs 16:9*   58

Roaring Like a Lion Sue Sherstad   *Proverbs 28:1*   60

Beloved Daughter Lisa Danegelis   *Song of Songs 2:4*   62

Little Foxes Nilda Campuzano   *Song of Songs 2:15*   64

God's Truth Transforms Our Lives Marlene Dawson   *Song of Songs 6:3a*   66

I Already AM Michelle Meade   *Isaiah 9:6*   68

A Friend Forever Lisa Danegelis   *Isaiah 41:8*   70

Taking a New Name Heidi Sampson   *Isaiah 43:1*   72

Rebuilding Heidi Sampson   *Isaiah 43:10a*   74

The Old Has Gone; The New is Here! Noreen Lessmann   *Isaiah 43:18-19*   76

Do Not Forget Kimberly Krueger   *Isaiah 46:9*   78

When Life is Messy, I Know Whose I Am Eleanor Weldie   *Isaiah 50:7*   80

By His Stripes Kimberly Krueger   *Isaiah 53:5b*   82

Invited to the Party Eleanor Weldie   *Isaiah 55:1-2b,3*   84

Shame Noreen Lessmann   *Isaiah 61:7*   86

He Calls Me Delightful Nilda Campuzano   *Isaiah 62:2, 4*   88

Life In the Potter's Hand Lisa Danegelis   *Isaiah 64:8*   90

Your Life is No Accident Susan Tyler   *Jeremiah 1:4-5*   92

Appointed Nilda Campuzano   *Jeremiah 1:9-10*   94

I Was Created for a Purpose Susan Tyler   *Jeremiah 29:11*   96

In Over My Head Heidi Sampson   *Ezekiel 2:1-2*   98

Table of Contents

Loving Mercy Heidi Sampson   *Micah 6:8*   100

Hind's Feet Sue Sherstad   *Habakkuk 3:19*   102

Free to Be Me Joni Jones   *Zephaniah 3:17*   104

The Smallest Steps Heidi Sampson   *Zechariah 4:10a*   106

The Say-So of God Michelle Meade   *Matthew 4:4*   108

Forgiveness Heather Taylor   *Matthew 6:14-15*   110

A Step In Faith Heather Taylor   *Matthew 6:16-19*   112

The Lord is My Provider Nilda Campuzano   *Matthew 6:31,32b*   114

The Gift Of Time Lisa Danegelis   *Matthew 7:11*   116

A House Divided Nilda Campuzano   *Matthew 12:25*   118

Growth Heather Taylor   *Matthew 13:1-9*   120

Who Do You Say I Am? Nilda Campuzano   *Matthew 16:13-15*   122

My Great Adventure Heather Taylor   *Mark 10:45*   124

Blessed is She Joni Jones   *Luke 1:45*   126

Peacefully Becoming Joni Jones   *Luke 8:48*   128

Authority Over the Power of the Enemy Susan Tyler   *Luke 10:19*   130

Childlike Faith Heidi Sampson   *Luke 12:32*   132

Listening to God Susan Tyler   *Luke 17:5-6*   134

Loved on Purpose Joni Jones   *John 3:16*   136

Pressing Forward Joni Jones   *John 5:8-9*   138

I Have Rivers of Living Water! Sue Sherstad · John 7:38 · 140

A New Definition of Success Eleanor Weldie · John 8:12 · 142

Stopping to Rest Heidi Sampson · John 13:6-7 · 144

Meet My Best Friend Heather Taylor · John 14:25-26 · 146

Stay Traci Weldie · John 15:4 · 148

From Head to Heart and Out into the World Amy Oaks · John 15:5-8 · 150

Joy Heather Taylor · John 15:11 · 152

My Father, My Friend Amy Oaks · John 15:15 · 154

With Confidence Luanne Nelson · John 17:11 · 156

No Longer That Way Joni Jones · Romans 5:8 · 158

Dead to the World Luanne Nelson · Romans 6:4 · 160

Servant of God Luanne Nelson · Romans 6:21-23 · 162

Flawless Joni Jones · Romans 8:1 · 164

Trust In ME Michelle Meade · Romans 8:14 · 166

A Cup of Grace Lisa Danegelis · Romans 8:15 · 168

God Loves Us as Much as He Loves Jesus Marlene Dawson · Romans 8:17 · 170

All Things Luanne Nelson · Romans 8:28 · 172

Triumph Over Every Trouble Sue Sherstad · Romans 8:37 · 174

Nothing Separates Us Noreen Lessmann · Romans 8:38-39 · 176

All We Need Lisa Danegelis · Romans 11:36 · 178

Yielding To The Will of God Sue Sherstad · Romans 12:1-2 · 180

The Test Heather Taylor · Romans 12:17-19 · 182

Table of Contents

You Already Have It Susan Brozek   *Romans 15:7*   184

Bound for Heaven's Shore Lisa Danegelis   *1 Corinthians 2:9*   186

My Favorite Body Part Traci Weldie   *1 Corinthians 3:16*   188

Messes Heidi Sampson   *1 Corinthians 15:10a*   190

Worse than My Worst Nightmare Kimberly Krueger   *1 Corinthians 15:57*   192

Vessels of Treasure Sue Sherstad   *2 Corinthians 4:6-7*   194

Who I'm Not Kimberly Krueger   *2 Corinthians 4:8-9*   196

Jesus Changes Everything Luanne Nelson   *2 Corinthians 5:17*   198

Representing Him Traci Weldie   *2 Corinthians 5:20*   200

You Can't Earn It Susan Brozek   *2 Corinthians 5:21*   202

God is a Good Father Noreen Lessmann   *2 Corinthians 6:18*   204

Blessed Noreen Lessmann   *2 Corinthians 8:9*   206

Run Your Race Kimberly Krueger   *2 Corinthians 10:12b*   208

My Weakness, His Masterpiece Tierney Gill   *2 Corinthians 12:9*   210

Loss Luanne Nelson   *2 Corinthians 12:10*   212

Jesus Loves Me This I Know Joni Jones   *Galatians 4:6*   214

I Am Free Michelle Meade   *Galatians 5:1*   216

No Regrets Heidi Sampson   *Galatians 6:9a*   218

He Chose Me! Sue Sherstad   *Ephesians 1:4*   220

I Am Who He Says I Am Heather Taylor   *Ephesians 1:11*   222

What Washes Away My Sin? Luanne Nelson	*Ephesians 1:7-8*	224
The Truth of Who You Are Sue Sherstad	*Ephesians 1:17-18*	226
Masterpiece Heather Taylor	*Ephesians 2:10*	228
When I Am Weak Susan Brozek	*Ephesians 3:16*	230
I am Loved Beyond Measure Susan Tyler	*Ephesians 3:18*	232
God Completes What He Begins Marlene Dawson	*Philippians 1:6*	234
Where Is My Home? Traci Weldie	*Philippians 3:20*	236
Strength Noreen Lessmann	*Philippians 4:13*	238
Crying Out for a Life Preserver Luanne Nelson	*Colossians 1:13*	240
The Cross Destroyed the Power of Sin Marlene Dawson	*Colossians 2:14*	242
Set Your Mind Sue Sherstad	*Colossians 3:1-2*	244
Power, Love, and Self Discipline Noreen Lessmann	*2 Timothy 1:7*	246
God's Love Restores Our Wholeness Marlene Dawson	*Hebrews 4:15-16*	248
God Equips the Called Noreen Lessmann	*Hebrews 13:20*	250
A Best Friend Susan Tyler	*James 2:23*	252
Chosen Joni Jones	*1 Peter 1:9*	254
God's Love Protects Us Marlene Dawson	*1 John 3:1-2*	256
Fearless Joni Jones	*1 John 4:18*	258
I Am An Overcomer Susan Brozek	*1 John 5:4*	260
I AM Everything Michelle Meade	*Revelation 1:8*	262
A New Name Kimberly Krueger	*Revelation 2:17b*	264

MAKING THE MOST OF
THIS DEVOTIONAL & JOURNAL

"A FEW Words on Your Identity in Christ," the third release in FEW International Publication's line of devotionals, is more than a book to simply read.

Seventeen dynamic authors from various age groups and walks of life share many of their personal identity struggles and insights. Their moving stories offer you hope and assure you that you are not alone in your quest to understand and walk in your true identity in Christ.

Each devotion is accompanied by an interactive journal page. This page begins with two introspective questions. Both the "Picture" and "Ask" sections will aid you in exploring and reflecting upon your identity journey by taking you deeper.

We encourage you to use the "Pray" section to turn the insight you've gained into a personal prayer you write back to the God. Your prayer can consist of thanking God for His Promises, declaring back to Him the treasure you've just attained, or to making your personal petition to Him. Or you can use this space to creatively express your heart to God through art.

Choose to work your way through each devotion at your own pace. Our writings and journal pages can be enjoyed in one sitting, or used over the course of two or three days.

If you like what you're reading within these pages, please let our Authors know! They love hearing from readers like you. Most FEW Authors are available to present to your ministry, group, church, or organization, too! Consider inviting one of our Authors to present a teaching on her devotion(s).

A FEW Words . . . we pray they are used powerfully in your life and on your journey to discover your true identity in Christ.

YOU SAY

You say I am loved when I can't feel a thing
You say I am strong when I think I am weak
And you say I am held when I am falling short
And when I don't belong, oh You say I am Yours
And I believe
Oh I believe
What You say of me
I believe
The only thing that matters now is everything You think of me
In You I find my worth, in You I find my identity

Songwriters: Jason Ingram / Paul Mabury / Lauren Daigle
You Say lyrics © Centricsongs, So Essential Tunes, SEE YOU AT THE PUB, 2018

Susan Brozek

Dear Reader,

Someone once said, "True beauty emanates from a person who boldly and unabashedly knows who he or she is in Christ."

How true this statement is! Knowing your identity in Christ is a topic that I have been passionate about for over 20 years, when I first opened my Christian psychotherapy practice. I began to discover, as I worked with my patients, that so many of them did not know how to answer the question, "Who are you?" I would receive well thought-out answers, but these answers would frequently surround their role and their performance in life (as in, "I'm a parent of 3 amazing children", "I'm the wife of an attorney", "I'm the lead supervisor at my job"). And at times, I would receive answers that touched on characteristics of themselves (as in, "I'm generous", "I'm a good listener", "I'm trustworthy"). While of course these statements were factual, and contained value and merit, they didn't incorporate who they were at their very core...in other words, who God created them to be!

So today I would ask you, dear reader, how would you answer the question..."Who are you?"

God's Word says in John 10:10, "The enemy of our soul has come to steal, kill, and destroy." Something that the devil relentlessly tries to steal from us as believers is our identity in Christ. He practices "identity theft"; he does not want us to know who we are in the Lord because if we do, that truth will transform us as we begin to learn in our minds and hearts how God views us!

Some people, as a result of upbringing or authority figures in their lives, can grow up believing they have very little value, or that they don't measure up, or are unlovable. What is spoken over a child during their formative years oftentimes determines what they live up to...or "down to", as the case may be. As an example, if you were told as a child that you could accomplish anything you set your mind to, you were set up to approach life with a sense of confidence in what you could try to achieve. On the other hand, if you were told that you would never amount to anything, it could have instilled in you a sense of inevitable failure, which may have strongly impacted you in such a way that it caused fear of trying new things or approaching new experiences. So as you can see, what you were "told" early on in your life is paramount in terms of how you see yourself as an adult. And this is where knowing who you are in Christ can completely transform your life!

As you study the list of Scriptural references of who you are in Christ included in this book, please choose to start believing what God Himself has "told" you; you can begin to embrace the worth and value that you have in Him simply by receiving who He has said you are. This is what I call "transformational truth"...truth that has the power to completely change how you see yourself, and as a result, how you live your life. At this point, you may be thinking, "I'd be really prideful if I believed all these verses about myself!" And my response to that is: no, you'd be defeated if you didn't! You're not who you are in Christ because of anything you have done; you are who you are in Christ because of what He has done, and His finished work at the Cross!

The purpose of this devotional book is to introduce you to all that you have inherited regarding your identity as a child of The King, and to begin to take that head knowledge about your identity in Christ and walk it out by pulling it into your heart. I encourage you to not only study the Scripture list, but to look up the verses, perhaps a few per day, and begin to meditate on what they mean for you in terms of how you see yourself.

It is my heartfelt prayer that as you begin to absorb the Scriptures which show you your identity in Christ through each devotion written, you would no longer look to others, to your job, to your achievements, or even to yourself, to determine your worth or value, but that you would come to look to God. May you see how much He loves you, and understand how valuable you are to Him...so that you can experience the abundant life that God has always longed for you to live!

In closing, I'd like to challenge you with the following concept: We are children of The King...therefore, which of these most honors our Savior? Failing to claim our rights and even doubting that they belong to us, or asserting our privilege as children of His royal family and claiming the rights that accompany our inheritance? Remember that God wants us to claim all that we have and all that we are in Him—it honors Him when we do so!

Let the One who created you be the One who defines you.

Prayers and Blessings as you discover who you are in Christ,

Susan C. Brozek, M.S.W., L.C.S.W.
Licensed Clinical Psychotherapist
Director/Founder, HEALING WORD PSYCHOTHERAPY SERVICES, LLC
www.healing-word.com • 414-254-9862
#1 Bestselling Author
TV Broadcast Show Host at The NOW Network
International Radio Broadcast Host, "The Way of Healing", at Reaching Out Radio Int'l

God Never Forgets By Marlene Dawson

God heard their groaning; and He remembered His covenant with Abraham, Isaac, and Jacob.
~ Exodus 2:24 (NIV)

Living in England when I was young allowed me to experience some of the best and some of the worst times of my life. We moved back to the United States less than a year after arriving because my mother caught my father abusing me. My father was not one to pay bills, so his refusal to pay storage fees caused us to lose many personal items, including my childhood pictures. Most of the items did not matter to me at the time, but when I was older I realized how precious those pictures from my childhood would be. It sometimes seemed as though parts of the first nine years of my life existed only in my memories. When my grandmother passed away, an aunt sent several pictures from my early years that mom sent to her mother. Some of the blanks of my childhood were finally sketched in. Even though I did not know that God knew me, He still gave me exactly what I needed. God always remembers His promises to me, and this is a great reminder of how precious I am to Him.

Most of us can relate to these groaning Israelites in Exodus 2:24. They have been slaves for four hundred years, awaiting their promised deliverer. They cried out to God, "Do You even remember us? Where is our deliverer?" This verse is part of Moses' story and his preparation for the deliverer position God placed on his shoulders. We will have difficult days and seasons in our lives, and God will reveal His loving kindness as we pursue Him, but He does not always answer as expected. God promised Abraham, Isaac, and Jacob that their descendants were His chosen people and He would always take care of them. Many of their descendants did not remember His promise, turning their backs on God. But God did not forget them! The Lord let His chosen people come to the end of themselves so they could realize their need for Him. The same is true today for all Christ-followers when we think we can figure out life for ourselves. Then we hit the wall of futility. "God, where are you? Don't you love me anymore?" We finally cry out to God and He moves on our behalf with His tender mercies. God remembers us, and He remembers each promise He has made to us.

Lord, You are my faithful Father who never forgets me.
Thank you, Lord! Amen.

I am Remembered

picture

What could you do to remember God's faithfulness to you?

ask

Tell about a time you hit the wall of futility waiting for God to answer.

pray

I am Remembered

God's Love Directs Us to Him By Marlene Dawson

Behold, I am going to send an angel before you to guard you along the way, and to bring you to the place which I have prepared. ~ Exodus 23:20 (NASB)

I attended a small women's retreat with an interesting beginning. Once everyone arrived, we were directed to a room where we chose a paper Scripture doily from a basket. You may have seen crocheted doilies on your grandmother's end tables when you were younger. As I opened my doily, I read how God would be sending an angel to guard me along my path. I was intrigued because I often wondered about the role of angels in a believer's life. God began uncovering what had been a mystery to me as I spent time in prayer, expanding my understanding and knowledge of angelic beings and their presence. I was excited to learn in Hebrews 1:14 that angels are God-sent messengers that help bring about God's will and purpose in our lives. One of the most exciting things I learned was God revealing He had sent an angel to guard me as He brought me to the place of accepting the invitation to join His family! The idea that God was present throughout my life, directing my steps to this place in time, is tenderly overwhelming! Exodus 23:20 was concrete evidence that God not only cared about me, but actively pursued me to become His daughter! I still have that paper doily more than thirty years later.

When God pursues us, we will process through issues and crises of faith. Learning to trust and believe God is worth every moment it takes, clinging to Him as His angels guide us along the path He planned for us. Without big and small tests, we will not have the testimonies that bring hope and encouragement to others. Our unique testimonies become the connection between our past, God's intervening salvation, and the change that comes from learning who we are in Christ. God desires to see us restored from our most painful experiences. He knows who will be impacted by our stories, so He leads us in ways that make each story relatable for others. His plan is to heal and restore us, so our stories can bring healing to others who have similar stories but don't yet have the hope of freedom in Christ. Exodus 23:20 assures us the truth is we can trust God with each step, or misstep, we take. He promises to protect us so we can arrive where He knows our lives will most impact others.

Lord God, I lay all of my brokenness before You to redeem and use to touch those who are desperate for You. Amen.

I am Directed

picture

Telling your story can help someone else get healing from their pain. Practice telling your story so you can be ready to speak when God opens that door.

ask

Share a time when you know God protected you, and how that brought you to where you are today.

pray

Abba's Heart By Michelle Meade

Do not be in dread or afraid of them. The Lord your God who goes before you will Himself fight for you, just as He did in Egypt before your eyes, and in the wilderness, where you have seen how the Lord your God carried you, as a man carries His son, all the way that you went until you came to this place, Yet in spite of this word you did not believe the Lord your God. ~ Deuteronomy 1:30-32 (ESV)

Perspective is everything. In my 30-year spiritual journey, God morphed from an angry, impersonal God into an adoring Father, Ever-Present Everything, and Bridegroom King. God didn't change. He never does. However, unresolved pain filtered and distorted His Word and the intent of His Heart. I couldn't see who God really was because my perspective was dredged in pain. The Children of Israel lived this truth for forty years! God commanded the Red Sea to disobey the laws of gravity and told ordinary cotton threads and leathered sandals to constantly reproduce! With every supernatural act, God tangibly expressed, "Because I AM, therefore I WILL." Yet, because they still carried the pain of their past, His Love didn't translate, let alone penetrate. The movie screens of their minds were stuck on rewind; re-playing the traumatic images of a lifetime of bondage. Haunting memories of the past overshadowed the miraculous unveiling of God's love in the present. He demonstrated His Father-hood in every possible way, yet they lived as orphans when they were Royal offspring. Often times this is how we feel when trained in adversity because we refuse to get past our pain to know the wonders of His Name. The Hebrew word for know is 'Yada' and means to know intimately by experience.

to know You in suffering - to know You in Glory
to know You as Everything - is our love story.

This was my heart's cry yet, in my journey to yada God, I have had difficulty even knowing what to call Him. It's like the awkward moment when you don't know whether to call your Father-in-Law Dad or by his first name. Is He The fierce Almighty or tender Father? His voice released every ounce of pretension, 'I AM not either or, I AM both and more ...

'I just long to hear your voice - I miss you don't you know
you used to climb upon My Knee - but that was long ago
Remember ME again - My Love's always the same
here I'll wait, don't hesitate - I'm calling out your name'
Copyright 2007 RememberMEmore.com

Papa, may Your loving Father's heart be forever graven upon mine. Amen.

I am His Girl

picture

God stops everything when He hears your voice call to Him.
He knows the warmth, intensity, and distinct sound of your heart.

ask

Do you feel safe addressing God as a loving Papa? Why or why not?

pray

Victory in the Battle By Lisa Danegelis

For the Lord your God is He who goes with you, to fight for you against your enemies, to save you.
~ Deuteronomy 20:4 (NKJV)

Two of my boys played football. Helmets clashed, limbs flailed and bodies fell. One of my sons, the defensive end, nicknamed "the hurricane" by opposing teams, was often a target. He would describe the violent mess at the bottom of the pile. Extra kicks, jabs, and demoralizing words ... anything to keep your opponent down. Until ... the player would rise, ball in hand ... victorious!

I've stood with my back to the wind, heels dug in and fists clenched as the battle raged in my own life. I knew I already had the victory. God doesn't lie. I believed it, I whispered it, I sang it. The very word was formed in the teardrops slinking down my cheeks. With William Wallace in the epic movie Braveheart, I screamed "FREEDOM!" The pain, the loss, the questions, the confusion, the sleepless nights and desperate days. The naysayers, the scoffers, the nightmares and trembling flesh ... it all tried to defeat me ... but failed. However. My God loved me too much ... I knew His love would win. God is in the end-zone cheering me on. I've been on the bottom of the pile for years, feeling invisible, battle-scarred and bruised. He watches. He smiles. He screams, "That's my girl!" He knows, in the end, my faith muscle will be stronger, my joy will shine brighter, my voice will be bolder, and my heart a bit larger. He also knew at the end, the crown of victory would be a bit too heavy for my head and that I would throw it at His feet anyway. We trusted each other.

Sometimes the God of love can seem like the God of loss. Life is often full of struggle, sorrow, and pain that can leave us in a state of disillusionment. But in His infinite wisdom, our Father knows there needs to be a battle before He can claim victory. With the right perspective, the battle can become a blessing to the surrendered soul. In the midst of it all, take the time to look ahead to the goal line and you will see God waving the flag of victory that He has already won for us. Establish yourself in that assured victory today, it's yours for the taking!

Thank you for Your ultimate sacrifice that won the victory for us. As I walk the path of life, help me to keep my eyes on the prize, Lord. Amen.

I am His Established

picture

Recall a time in your life when you were in the middle of a battle. How did God bring you out of it? What did He reveal about Himself through your struggles?

ask

Can you believe God already has the victory in every battle? Can you believe you are victorious?

pray

Sweet Dreams By Heather Taylor

The Lord himself goes before you and will be with you; he will never leave you nor forsake you. Do not be afraid; do not be discouraged. ~ Deuteronomy 31: 8 (NIV)

As a child, I had bad nightmares. Overwhelmed with fear each night, I eventually stopped sleeping altogether until my body would pass out from sheer exhaustion. I would try to fall asleep before my parents would shut the living room TV off, a sign that they were going to bed. If I could manage to nod off before they went to bed, I wouldn't have to feel loneliness envelop me when they shut their bedroom door for the night. Sleep and feeling safe died with the sound of their bedroom door closing. As an adult, my childish nightmares faded and fear took on a new life, a constant companion named anxiety. We got along pretty well, considering, but once I became pregnant with my first child, all bets were off. Anxiety brought a friend to stay and her name was worry! I spent my days worrying about what could go wrong and my nights filled with fear, wondering when the things I worried about would happen.

One morning, I awoke to the sound of the television. I was angry, I had just fallen asleep when I heard the man on the screen asking, "Are you letting the devil steal your joy? Do you spend your days worrying about things you can't change?" My ears perked up and I found myself answering the TV, "Yes, yes I do!" The television voice continued, "You don't have to live in fear anymore. In the Name of Jesus, I rebuke Satan out of your mind right now and I will tell you he has no right to be there. You are a child of God and he has no business making you fear anything."

I laid my head on the pillow and said a little prayer. "Lord, if it's true that you can get rid of my fear, I ask you, Jesus, to please remove this from my heart. I beg You, Lord, to save me from this dread I feel all the time." To my surprise, I slept the entire night. I never had a problem with fear keeping me awake again! God was making me unafraid before I even knew that was a part of my new identity in Christ!

Lord God, I ask You to deliver me from the temptation to give in to fear, worry, and anxiety. I ask You right now, in Jesus' Name, to help me "let go and let God." I cast my cares upon You Lord and I know that you will remove this burden from me, for Your Word says that You have gone before me and that I have nothing to fear. Amen.

I am Unafraid

picture

What if you could let go of fear, worry, and anxiety and let God take care of it? What would be different in your days and nights?

ask

Do you find yourself worrying about things you cannot control? What does the Bible say about worry?

pray

Watch Your Six! By Nilda Campuzano

Look to the Lord and his strength; seek His face always. Remember the wonders he has done, his miracles, and the judgments he pronounced. ~ 1 Chronicles 16:11-13 (NIV)

I have the privilege of working with people involved in law enforcement. Prior to special operations, the team comes together for a briefing session. This session gives them exact details of the position they are assigned to, what is expected of them during the operation and all pertinent information regarding their targets. When the briefing is over and everyone is heading out to the streets, I often hear them say to each other, "Watch your six!" which simply means "watch your back!"

Recently, as I was examining certain areas of my life that are out of alignment with my identity in Christ, this phrase popped into my head: "Watch your six." It came not as a warning, but as an invitation to look back for a moment and analyze my past. It was also an invitation to stop asking God to change me into something different and instead go back to being who I used to be, before fear and negative thinking got the best of me.

Throughout my life, I have experienced God's deliverance and supernatural provision, but it is said that forgetting is the natural state of our mind - it is remembering that takes effort. In the Old Testament, the Israelites are exhorted time and time again to remember the wonders and miracles God had done, and to proclaim them to the new generations, a practice that remains today. "Watch your six!"

Looking back at my life, I realized that I spent too much time asking God to "get me out of here!" Instead of trying to flee a situation, God calls me to stand on who I am already. God says that my victory is not on becoming somebody new, but in recognizing who I am; my victory does not lie on what God could do, but in remembering what He has already done. Sometimes our victory is not ahead, but behind; not in who we can become, but in who we ceased to be; not in what we can do, but in what we stopped doing when we became His.

God Almighty, grant me the grace to recall all the wonders you have performed in my life; bring me back to a place of complete gratitude, not just for what you will do in my life, but for everything you have already done. Amen.

I am Focused

picture

Chose and area of your life where you need a breakthrough. Meditate not on what you should do, but what you stopped doing. Write down your revelations.

ask

What wonders and miracles God has done in my life am I forgetting to recall? List your blessings.

pray

I am Focused

The Golden Scepter By Kimberly Krueger

When the king noticed Queen Esther standing in the entry court, he was pleased. The king held out to Esther the gold scepter in his hand, and she came forward and touched the scepter's tip. Then the king said to her, "What is it, Queen Esther? What do you want? I'll give you anything—even half the kingdom."
~ Esther 5:2-3 (NASB)

My Golden Scepter is extended to you. Ask Me for anything. Could I be hearing correctly? I was at the end of a 3-day fast and just finished reading Esther 5:2 when I heard the Spirit say this to me. How could God be offering to me what the King offered Esther? Was I imagining this? Confirmation came two ways: His Presence filled the room externally, and an overwhelming sense of His deep love flooded my insides. Before I knew it, I was face down on the floor.

Indeed, He was extending His favor to me. "But Lord, why me?" I was so blown away that I was chosen to have my own "Esther" moment in His Court. He skipped over my questions and prompted me: *Ask Me for anything.* He was kind but insistent. I wasn't going to squander this opportunity; I would choose my words carefully. My first request echoed King Solomon's when he asked for wisdom to lead God's people. The Lord urged me to ask for more. "More? Really?" I remembered Joyce Meyer's words and echoed her. "I'd rather ask God for everything and get some of it than ask Him for nothing and get all of it." I asked Him for everything, and He asked me to be more specific. I told him through sobs and tears what "everything" meant to me: every promise He ever made me. Every promise in His Word. I poured out every desire until I was undone, and I was overwhelmed by His "Yes."

I've pondered that day many times. Did the God of the universe really offer me anything that belongs to Him? Yes, He did, and He is offering it to you, too. Friend, Esther's story is your story. It paints a picture of Christ, our King, and His chosen Bride. You are His Esther and He has extended His golden scepter of favor to you, by way of the Cross. You've been chosen out of obscurity, like Esther, and invited to state your requests to the most benevolent King who will ever live! You stand in His court with His golden scepter perpetually extended to you because your King favors you! Will you reach out and touch it, as Esther did? Will you boldly ask? I hope you say yes because you were made for such a time as this. (Esther 4:14)

Lord, give me the courage and faith to be Your Esther and receive my heart's desires because of Your favor and generosity. Amen.

I am Favored

picture

Picture yourself standing in Heaven's Courts with Jesus extending His Golden Scepter to you. Describe that scene. What do you see, hear, think, feel?

ask

What would you ask Him for if He said to you, "Ask Me for anything!"

pray

Full of Doubt By Heidi Sampson

Though He slay me, yet I will hope in Him. ~ Job 13:15a (NIV)

Since the day we met our boys in foster care, they have been unsure of who God is. Trauma has skewed their view of spirituality. In the eyes of my children, God allowed their lives to begin in an unsafe home. Perceiving God as Father is a tough concept for kids who have been abandoned, neglected, and abused.

The view my adopted kids have of God as an unconditionally loving Father lands on my shoulders because the first set of parents screwed up.

That is hard to accept some days for a Christian parent, but forcing them to love a God they cannot trust only pushes them further away. I am a strong believer that their doubts have merit. Who am I to tell my kids that they shouldn't blame God for the awful things they experienced? We share Truth with them, but they don't come to love Jesus by refuting their difficult questions and doubts about God's goodness.

We do all of our "normal" religious rituals to expose them to our family foundation in Christ. But God must answer their questions and doubts in His own, real way. Deep in my heart, I want them to see just how truly good My King is. I know that is the only way my two precious boys will heal.

So when our boys have trudged their way through yet another church service, we began to sing these words: "I am chosen, not forsaken. I am who You say I am. You are for me, not against me. I am who You say I am." I brought them close and reminded them of the promises they were singing. That God is present in their lives, and accepting His identity is the only way to move forward from their pasts. Those words ring true in my own heart as someone who has been redeemed by the Savior. But those words coming from the mouths of my wounded, broken, chaotic, once fatherless children. That is redemption and evidence of God's goodness. Looking at the beginning of our kids' lives, it is easy to be skeptical of who God is. When life is complicated, it can feel as if God has forgotten you. We must remember that we cannot see the whole picture while God in His sovereignty can. We go forward in the hope that He gives us.

Lord, help my unbelief. When I doubt and question Your presence, remind me that You have not forgotten me. Help me to trust Your redemption in my life. Amen.

I am Hopeful

picture

List your doubts about God. List things you are bitter about. Ask Him to reveal Himself to you.

ask

Becoming bitter about something can be evidence that there is a lack of faith in God's plan. What are the areas in your life you have become hardened to and doubt God?

pray

Safe & Secure in My Savior's Shadow By Tierney Gill

I will both lay me down in peace, and sleep; for thou, LORD, only makest me dwell in safety. ~ Psalm 4:8

Three-hundred-sixty-five. This number is not just the total days in a year, but it's the number of times the Bible tells us to "fear not" or "do not be afraid." Arguably, we are given this command juxtaposed with a corresponding promise for each day of the year. Clearly, God does not want us to have a spirit of fear because as His children, we are loved. We are secure. We are safe.

Safety was a fleeting ideal in my childhood. I grew up in the inner city, in the violent northside ghetto of Milwaukee, Wisconsin, where idyllic images of safety and security were non-existent. Our property was routinely vandalized. Gang violence, pimping and prostitution, drug trafficking and more hung out on our street corners, lived next door to us, surrounded us on all sides. My siblings and I were not allowed to go outside to even take the garbage out without another sibling right there watching us. We had the police over so many times that we were all on a first-name basis.

The little we could do to protect ourselves, we did. We had an alarm system. We put up a fence. We kept a firearm in the house. We even got two German Shepherds. But we weren't under any illusions: we all knew Who was keeping us safe. None of those measures explained how a bullet meant for Mom instead shot out the car passenger window behind her head. It wasn't our doing that protected my parents one night when they were trapped in gang crossfire, huddled on the floor of our family van, hearing bullets hitting the car while cut off from their unprotected kids in the house yards away.

My life and the lives of my family are a testament to the truth that our God protects us. Our safety, and peace, was and is of the Lord alone. In Him, I was and am protected and cared for - I don't have a reason to fear, but I have plenty of reasons to trust! The image that David paints in Psalm 4 is that I can trust my Heavenly Father so much in the middle of the all-encompassing dangers that like a child, I can lie down in peace and enjoy a restful sleep knowing that in Him I am safe, protected, loved, and secure.

Father, I thank you for the peace and security that is in Christ.
You command me to not be afraid but to trust in You and
rest securely in Your love. Amen.

I am Secure

picture

How can you take this Scripture passage and embrace the peace and safety that is yours in Christ, learning to "fear not" in the midst of this tumultuous world?

ask

What are some examples you see in your life of times that God has protected you?

pray

I am Secure

Don't Talk About My Daughter Like That! By Kimberly Krueger

How I love you, Lord! You are my defender. The Lord is my protector; he is my strong fortress. My God is my protection, and with him I am safe. He protects me like a shield; he defends me and keeps me safe ~ Psalm 18:1-2 (GNT)

I was in my closet getting dressed while mentally reviewing—no rating myself on—how I did during a recent conversation with an important person. It wasn't looking good for me; the judge in this courtroom (me) was merciless. The verdict was in before I even got my pants on. Ugh. You sounded so dumb. Why did you say that? What is your problem? What were you thinking? YOU'RE SO STUPID! And there it was—old faithful—the most rehearsed verdict in the courtroom that is my head. But court wouldn't be dismissed until I berated myself out loud. So, all alone in my closet, I brought down my gavel with this rebuke: "KIM YOU ARE SO STUPID!" Instantly, I heard the Voice of the Lord. It was firm. Authoritative. "HEY! DON'T TALK ABOUT MY DAUGHTER LIKE THAT!"

Eek! I was in trouble; I knew it. Like a little girl shrinking back from her father's booming voice, I retreated. But only for a second because I quickly realized... He's actually defending me ... He's protecting me ... from me! Fear was cast out instantly by His perfect love and David's words from Psalm 18 became my own personal revelation. "How I love you, Lord! You are my defender. The Lord is my protector ..." Even if He has to protect me from me.

Can I tell you the secret formula to identity? What you believe you are, you will become. That's it. It's that easy ... and that hard. The thoughts we think are the single largest factor that determines our identity. What we believe determines how we behave which determines who we become. So, God scolded me to alert me to the danger and destruction lurking in my thoughts and words. He protects me from me because He loves me and knows exactly where the opposition to my true identity begins and ends—in my mind.

This is why Romans 12:2 says to "let God transform you into a new person by changing the way you think." (NLT) We need His help because WE are the biggest threat to our identity in Christ—the minds we possess and the tongues that do their bidding are a more formidable foe than all the lies from the devil himself. But take heart! Philippians 1:6 promises us that the God "who began this good work in you, will carry it on until it is finished," even if it means protecting you from you.

Dear Lord, thank You for saving me from me! How I love You, Lord. Renew my thinking today, and expose every thought that opposes my true identity in You. Amen.

I am Defended

picture

Your mind is the battlefield where the fight for your identity takes place. What beliefs are fighting against each other?

ask

Do you need God to protect you from you?

pray

I am Defended

He Leads in Paths of Righteousness By Sue Sherstad

He makes me lie down in [fresh, tender] green pastures; He leads me beside the still and restful waters. He refreshes and restores my life (my soul); He leads me in the paths of righteousness [uprightness and right standing with Him - not for my earning it but] for His name's sake. ~ Psalm 23:2-3 (AMP)

As a teenager growing up on a farm, one of my chores was tending sheep. Every morning I led them out to pasture following a path to feed on green grass and drink crystal cold water from the bubbly stream flowing through the fields. The sheep knew my voice and came running when I called out at dusk, "Here, Lamby-Lamby!" They followed me to the safety of the shed as darkness settled in.

These wonderful memories of my childhood helped me to embrace the revelation of Jesus as my Shepherd when I first came to know Him. He is a loving Savior and the Good Shepherd of our souls. He desires to lead us on "paths of righteousness" that align with the destiny He has planned for us.

This verse came alive to me during a counseling session with my pastor. He was praying over me to break off an oppressive spirit when the Lord gave him a vision of me standing on the bottom rung of a very high ladder. Each rung represented a scheme or plot the devil was planning for my future. Above the ladder appeared a bright laser beam of fire that cut the ladder in half with explosive power from top to bottom. As the ladder split in half, the rung I was standing on fell away. The Lord set my feet down on a new path that appeared before me. This new path of righteousness led me to know Jesus as the lover and restorer of my soul, and His plans for my life.

Did you know that if you don't seek the Lord for His plans for your life, the devil has plans for you? His plans for you are evil and for destruction. Jesus has a plan to prosper you and not to harm you. His path of righteousness leads to the abundant life that He died to give you to fulfill the plan uniquely designed for you. Colossians 1:10 TPT says, "We pray that you would walk in the ways of true righteousness, pleasing God in every good thing you do. Then you'll become fruit-bearing branches, yielding to His life, and maturing in the rich experience of knowing God in His fullness!" As you follow your Shepherd in paths of righteousness, you will fulfill His plans for your life, bearing the fruit of righteousness for His Glory.

Lord, I Praise You! You are the Good Shepherd. Lead me in paths of righteousness so that I may know the plans that you have for me. Amen.

I am Led

picture

How would you put walking in "paths of righteousness" in your own words?

ask

What is the spirit leading you to do in obedience to this passage?

pray

I am Led

Taste and See By Michelle Meade

Taste and see that The Lord is good. Oh the joys of those who take refuge in Him! ~ Psalm 34:8 (NLT)

The first thing God did in Eden was lay out an extravagant spread of food. His kids didn't have to pay or work the land; all they had to do was stay away from a singular forbidden tree. Imagine the adventure of tasting and seeing God is good with every delectable drip of juice that lingered on their tongue. Satan knew his only chance was to interrupt their feast. Hence the slithering liar seduced them into handing over their birthright.

The Fall of our first parents and our fall is the same shift from God to self. There are still two trees in The garden of our heart, the Tree of Thee and the Tree of Me. Every single time I put my adoring gaze on God and choose to eat from His tree, I'm nourished with Life as I receive His love as my portion. But every time I turn and choose to look inward instead of upward I have to search for my own provision and fulfillment. Doesn't sound so dangerous at first. After all, how hard is it to find something to sustain us? Fast food alternatives fill the inward cavity; Facebook and Instagram spike our self-worth with the approval of friends and followers. But the satisfaction and sympathy expire with that day's social media cycle. The next time your soul growls with hunger pains and reaches to grab a substitute, hear God beckon you to partake of His everlasting love. He aches to satisfy your longing soul with Life.

'taste and see that I AM God - the First, The Last, The Same
drink and eat, I'll complete the work for which I came
Living waters flow - deep within My Vine
fruit of My Flesh your skin's made fresh to carry My New Wine
everlasting Marriage - by own Blood we're bound
I'll never leave, to My Word cleave - your heart's now Holy Ground'
Copyright 2007 RememberMEmore.com

Holy Spirit, I'm grateful for those who have fed me the Word, but my earnest desire is to be satisfied in You alone, eating directly from Your hand. Amen.

I am Satisfied

picture

The Father loves His children equally. You are loved as much as the most renowned prophet or preacher, past or present.

ask

Is that reality hard to accept? Why or why not?

pray

I am Satisfied

Beautifully Broken By Tierney Gill

The righteous cry, and the LORD heareth, and delivereth them out of all their troubles. The LORD is nigh unto them that are of a broken heart; and saveth such as be of a contrite spirit. Many are the afflictions of the righteous; but the LORD delivereth him out of them all. ~ Psalm 34:17-19

You're beautifully broken, and you can be whole again
Even a million scars, doesn't change whose you are
You're worthy. Beautifully broken.

I have loved the refrain of the above song, Beautifully Broken, by Plumb since I first heard it. To me, the song title and reinforced message seemed to be a misnomer, an impossible contradiction. Broken-ness certainly is many things - ugly, degrading, hurtful, hateful - but not beautiful! At least, that is what I believed, and it dragged me further into the depths of despair as I reeled from the constant pain and pressure of physical ailments, failed and abusive relationships, emotional damage, and more. Angry and hurting, I lashed out at those around me, at God even, as the pain became too heavy, the scars too deep, the seeming abandonment too real to bear alone.

None of us like to live in our brokenness. Pain is not a pleasant experience, and the lonely weariness of a grieving heart is especially difficult to bear. Yet, I am learning that even from something hard, God can and does create beauty. Carbon, in its basest and most broken form, when subjected to tremendous heat and pressure, produces scintillating diamonds. When some outside force that doesn't belong there—an irritant—enters the soft skin of a mollusk, it causes a wound. The mollusk then secretes nacre, layer upon layer, over that scar, in a years-long self-protection and healing process that produces a dazzling pearl.

God hears my cries and is delivering me out of my troubles and afflictions, as the psalmist reflects. And as Plumb's song testifies to, every tear, doubt, fear and regret we encounter, points to the fact that our brokenness is, in fact, a thing of beauty. That doesn't mean the process itself is easy! Where I, in my pain see only my scars and wounds, God allows others to see a pearl. Where I see only my brokenness, God wills me patience to see the diamond that He is busily crafting, that I may radiate His love and light to a darkened world. He is near me. He will deliver me. He is weaving together my broken pieces, my heartaches, hardships, and hurts, into beautiful jewels fit to adorn the crown of my Lord and King.

Heavenly Father, Thank You for Your promises of restitution and deliverance. I know that You are near me, hear my cries, and feel my pain as Your own. Help me to trust in You even as I cry out for Your continued deliverance. Amen.

I am Beautifully Broken

picture

What areas of brokenness might God be leading you to surrender to Him?

ask

What does beautifully broken mean to you?

pray

I am Beautifully Broken

He Inclined to Me By Sue Sherstad

I waited patiently and expectantly for the Lord; and He inclined to me and heard my cry. He drew me up out of a horrible pit [a pit of tumult and of destruction], out of the miry clay, and set my feet upon a Rock, steadying my steps and establishing my goings. ~ Psalm 40:1-2 (AMP)

I have come to know Jesus as my Deliverer. He has been faithful to answer my call in every circumstance. When I came to the Lord over 30 years ago, I was in a horrible pit of oppression from demonic forces after being raped and assaulted. Paralyzing fear and nightmares plagued me at night. I dreaded to go to bed never knowing if this was going to be another one of "those nights."

My journey to deliverance began when I learned to wait upon Him. To wait in Hebrew means, "in waiting I waited." That is, I continued to wait, and I learned to be earnest and persevere in prayer! His Word says, "He inclined to me," which means to bow. My heavenly Father bowed to place His ear near my mouth and heard me call to Him. He turned Himself favorably toward me because of my persevering prayer. He heard my prayers for help and raised me up out of the pit I was in.

Romans 10:13 promises "For whosoever calls upon the Lord shall be saved." To save in the Greek is "Sozo" and means to deliver or protect; heal and restore health, be made whole, to keep safe and sound, to rescue from danger or destruction. That's what Jesus did for me. He rescued me! He relocated me from the kingdom of darkness into the Kingdom of Light! I met my loving Heavenly Father and developed an intimate relationship with Him in the Secret Place. He set my feet on the Rock of Jesus Christ and ordered my steps into His plan for my life. He put a new song in my mouth, a song of praise for His Goodness!

We've all been there, enduring the painfully long wait for that breakthrough that we are so desperate for, waiting expectantly for an answer from Heaven to rush in and rescue. Whether we are waiting for His healing touch, a financial breakthrough or deliverance from bondage, no matter what your "pit" may be, He is Faithful to hear your cry and bring deliverance.

Heavenly Father, I praise You because You are my deliverer. I trust in Your saving power to heal, to restore, to protect and rescue me. Set my feet on the Rock and lead me into your perfect will. I wait upon You to answer me. In Jesus' Name! Amen.

I am Heard by Him

picture

In what way is the Holy Spirit speaking to you in waiting upon the Lord?

ask

How has Jesus revealed Himself as deliverer in your life and shown you that He inclines His ear to you?

pray

I am Heard by Him

Winding Roads By Sue Sherstad

A father of the fatherless and a judge and protector of widows is God in His holy habitation. God places the solitary [the lonely] in families and gives the desolate a home in which to dwell; He leads the prisoners out to prosperity; but the rebellious dwell in a parched land. ~ Psalm 68:5-6 (AMP)

Life is a journey that takes us down many winding roads and through many seasons. Some bring joy and others, sorrow. Early in my journey with the Lord, I was alone in the season of singleness. I came home from work to a lonely apartment greeted by my little dog. Being almost 30, I thought my life would be different! My brother and sisters were married with children, which put panic in my heart for fear that I had "missed it." Dating and painful breakups added to my loneliness with each failed relationship. Anxiousness gripped my heart with the fear of being alone.

Then came the turn-around! The Lord led me to a little church in the country where He changed my life. I grew in the knowledge of who I was in Christ as His child in the family of God. My focus turned to living my life for Jesus. The Lord gave me a prophetic word. "If you will be faithful where I have planted you, I will bring your husband to you." I clung tightly to this, trusting that the Lord would do what He said. As I read Psalm 68:6, "God places the solitary in families," hope came to my heart that my dream would come to pass. Six years later, the fulfillment of the Lord's promise walked through the doors of my little church on a Sunday morning. Dan Sherstad, a single pastor came from Chicago to preach at my little church in the cornfield. We dated and were married later that year when I was 36 years old. I'm blessed with the beautiful family that I believed God for. Through this journey I learned that the Lord is with me, I am not alone.

No matter the season you're in, He is with you. You are His child, chosen and adopted into His family. He heals the orphan heart with His unconditional love and acceptance. He promises to never leave you or forsake you. He defends the widow and promises to be your husband. He gives hope to the prisoner, His mercy and grace bring redemption and restoration. To the lonely, He gives a family. Take courage and find strength and comfort in His unfailing love. In every season, He is with you. You are not alone!

Heavenly Father, I praise You knowing I am not alone. You are with me in every season of my life. Give me courage and strength as I trust in Your loving care for me. In Jesus' Name! Amen.

I am Not Alone

picture

How does this passage bring hope and encouragement to you?

ask

What would be an example of " I am not alone" that you see in your life?

pray

I am Not Alone

At My Lowest By Heidi Sampson

The Lord is compassionate and gracious, slow to anger, abounding in love. ~ Psalm 103:8 (NIV)

Our son was adopted at age seven, and due to many life circumstances, he struggles with making good choices. My husband and I were called to one particularly bad situation at school that caused him to be suspended. As we drove him home, my first parental instinct was to correct and rebuke—to be mad at him or embarrassed by his actions. But I could not. He was so deep in shame that he did not understand why he was even alive. He hunched over on the ground and refused to look at us.

When I look past his misbehavior and hear the quiet, scared voice behind the yelling and dramatics, I am awakened to see the depth of my son's feelings. He is overwhelmed with regret and sorrow over his choices. He whispers things like, "if I wasn't so stupid," or "if I was a better person." I know that he understands right from wrong and has the ability to treat people well. He knows there are conse- quences for his actions, but on that day, the emotion of shame overcame his slim frame. He could not physically or mentally comprehend the value he brings to this life. He could not see outside his own choice. So, above correcting, my first job as his mom is to reassure my son that this awful choice is not who he is. I am determined to respond with compassion.

This reminds me of my Heavenly Father's love. When I am at my lowest and I do not think I contribute anything of worth, His first instinct is not to give a to-do list. He embraces me and He puts aside all of my failures to make sure I understand how loved I am. What my son does not realize is that he was not adopted for what he has done or what his potential is. We brought him into our family simply because he exists. And that is what Jesus does for me. It is simply my existence that causes Him to love me without conditions. No matter the mess I have made, God's first response is one purely of love.

Father, thank You for loving my existence. Thank You for embracing me, even at my worst. Give me eyes to see myself as valuable as You find me to be. Allow me to be loving towards others before I jump to anger. Amen.

I am *Unconditionally Loved*

picture

How would your life be different if you embodied God's response of love and compassion before anger?

ask

What about yourself do you think will exclude you from God's love?

pray

I am Unconditionally Loved

Under Construction By Nilda Campuzano

Unless the Lord builds the house, its builders labor in vain. ~ Psalm 127:1 (NIV)

It is said that Wisconsinites experience two seasons: winter and construction. I must admit I tend to be very impatient when it comes to road construction; as much as I enjoy the finished product, I dislike the process. If I had it my way, construction would only happen at night, when I am not using the roads at all.

Recently, I realized I was under heavy construction myself. Life, as I knew it, was crumbling, and I felt powerless to stop the impending wrecking ball that was threatening to crush everything I had built for the past six years.

One early morning, feeling completely overwhelmed to face the day, I finally let it all out; I cried out to God. I spewed all my frustration, asking Him why was He taking away everything He gave me; why was He destroying everything He built. I seldom claim to hear from God, but I heard the phrase "I didn't build this!" so clearly, so decisively, it stopped my rant at once. I was suddenly overcome with such clarity.

In the midst of my grief I realized God didn't build this life, I did. Every day I asked Him to just give me life, I would take care of the rest, and He obliged. Without a blueprint, the proper foundation, or even the right material, I built my life out of fear, hurt, and disappointment. It was a house made of straw, sitting on sand. When the winds blew and the rains came, I found myself exposed and grieving for the loss.

"Unless the Lord builds the house," whispered the solution. If the Lord builds the house, it will be built to last. I extended my hands and wholeheartedly presented all the broken pieces to God with a humble heart. I asked Him to take my feeble attempts at building and make it all new. I am trusting that as He rebuilds my heart, mind, soul, and life, He'll cement it all together upon The Rock. I believe all the pieces of my life will come together as a powerful testimony that The Master Builder is still doing what He does best: building. And for the first time ever, I am perfectly happy with construction season!

Eternal Creator, I surrender the need to plan and control every area of my life; I understand that your plans are better than mine, I rest safe and secure knowing Your blueprint is better than anything I could design on my own. Amen.

I am Being Built

picture

As you examine your life, which area could use a remodeling from the Master Builder and why?

ask

The Bible teaches us that we are co-creators with God; as you reflect in your life, how has God shown you that His ways are better than your ways? What have you co-created with Him?

pray

I Am Content By Michelle Meade

O Lord, my heart is not lifted up; my eyes are not raised too high; I do not occupy myself with things too great and too marvelous for me. But I have calmed and quieted my soul like a weaned child with its mother; like a weaned child is my soul within me. O Israel, hope in the Lord, from this time forth and forevermore. ~ Psalm 131:1-2 (ESV)

Contentment is cultivated by learning to do without what we thought we needed, until we realize Who we have is already enough. I understood this concept during the process of weaning my children. When they needed nourishment or comfort I stopped everything and held them close to my heart. In this safe place of provision they were taught to trust in my love. Once teeth were cut, it was time to transition to solid food and with each refusal to let them nurse came severe protest. My heart would ache because they didn't yet understand "no, not this, but this..." was necessary for growth. The love and trust they experienced for over a year were being tested.

"Mama, how dare you not give me what I crave in my safe place?" was silently expressed as little hands tore at my blouse and tears fell onto my chest. God trains us to trust in His love similarly. He provides everything we need as spiritual infants, but as we mature, little by little, we are taught Kingdom principles through dire need. Like our transitioning toddlers, we pull back and pull fits and demand we be given everything we think we need. But it is His Father's heart of love that says "no, not this, but this." These growing pains enlighten us and enlarge our capacity to receive what our souls truly crave. Every time we climb upon His lap we are being trained in shalom; to be content, completely safe and sound as beloved daughters of the Most High God, regardless of what life throws our way. That's when we know I AM THAT I AM is a good Father who cherishes us, down to the very hairs on our head.

'do not fret or be dismayed - your provision has been made
be content and do not fear - for I AM is always here
though circumstances may be tough - lift up your eyes ... I AM ENOUGH'
Copyright 2007 RememberMEmore.com

Papa! Empower me to ride with joyous wonder upon the crashing waves; what evil intended to break me, Your glorious hand has used to make me. I'm so thankful and content to be Your girl. Amen.

picture

Jesus slept content during the storm, secure in His Father's heart.

ask

What would it look like to rest in God's love in the middle of your raging storms?

pray

I am Content

No More Hiding By Eleanor Weldie

O Lord, you have searched me and known me! ~ Psalm 139:1 (ESV)

"Oh, cool," I faked a smile, trying to sound supportive as my friend showed me his new tattoo. A half-dollar sized rocket was taking off from his left calf, rainbow-colored smoke trailing behind as it plunged up his leg. He was very proud of it. "Um, why did you get it?" I asked, hoping the backstory would shed some light on this interesting choice.

"I like space?" He sounded hurt. "Neat!" I forced out. Let me be clear: I am not against tattoos. I myself have some and I think they can look beautiful and be incredibly meaningful. But for as long as I had known my friend, I had never heard him talk about space or rocket ships. He cleared up my confusion. "I'm getting lots of small pieces right now to showcase different parts of my identity – what I like and who I am." Now it made sense. This kind of patchwork artistry was becoming more popular in tattoo culture. Lots of tiny, graphic tattoos cover people's arms and legs to show off their interests. And, while I enjoy the look, I disagree that it showcases one's identity.

Our identities are not a collection of our likes and dislikes. While our interests, talents, and personalities inform our identities, they are not what make us who we are. Our identity is found inside our souls, in the innermost parts of ourselves; and those intangibles are often much harder to tattoo on our bodies.

I know I can often feel like I can't show my true identity because I believe it has been tainted by past mistakes or shame. I would never want to advertise that part of me. It is in times like this that I remember there is One who already knows my identity perfectly, and still loves me. My Lord has me tattooed on His heart. He created me; He knows when I have fallen; He knows my deepest desires; He is working to create a pure heart in me. He has searched me and knows the deepest parts of my identity. I can remember and be comforted in the fact that He loves me as I am – tattoos and all.

Lord, You have searched me and know me. I often try to hide anything but perfection from the world, but You already have seen my imperfections. You love me through it all, and You keep bestowing grace upon me. Help me live fully alive in the knowledge that I am loved! Amen.

I am Known

picture

How can you begin to live in the knowledge that your past mistakes and failures no longer hold you back?

ask

What parts of your identity are you ashamed of or want to hide? What does it feel like to know God already has seen this part of you and loves you fully?

pray

I am known

Mistake or Masterpiece? By Amy Oaks

For you created my inmost being; you knit me together in my mother's womb. I praise you because I am fearfully and wonderfully made. ~ Psalm 139:13-14 (NIV)

I was a mistake. I did the math, and I was born almost exactly seven months after my parents were married. They were just 19 years old; barely 20 when I was born. They had a shotgun wedding, lived in a tiny cheap apartment—cleaned and managed the building to pay the rent, and never finished college. My dad has an aptitude for drawing and dreamed of moving to California to become a car designer. My mom earned great grades and could have been the first in her family to earn a college degree. Because of me, they were instead catapulted into adulthood together and learned their lessons in the school of hard knocks. Because of me, my parents lost their freedom and innocence.

I'm not saying I wasn't loved. My parents were blessed to be closely surrounded by family, so some of my best memories from early childhood are of my grandmothers taking care of me while my parents worked. They did their best, making sure I had all I needed including attention and care. Still, what if I had never been born? Would they have fulfilled their life goals and dreams beyond having a family? Would my mother have had the wedding of her dreams? Would my parents have even married at all?

I suppose I could dwell on these things and live my life as if I really am a mistake; the result of a date-night decision gone wrong. Or, I could remember that I really am fearfully and wonderfully made ... on purpose with a purpose! My life hasn't been perfect. God never promised us that. This world overflows with sin and evil, as well as love and good intentions. God gifted me this life all mapped out in advance for me to live. He put people and events in my life so I can fulfill His perfect plan. It doesn't matter how I got here or what baggage I bring. I am ready and willing to live this life as He intended for me. I am not a mistake, but His masterpiece!

Dear Lord, help me see myself as You see me – perfectly created to fulfill Your purposes for me on this earth, in this life. Remind me that I can be a blessing to those around me without being perfect. In Your Name I pray, Amen.

I am Wonderfully Made

picture

What would your life look like if you viewed it from God's perspective instead of your own?

ask

Does God make mistakes?

pray

I am Wonderfully Made

Healed Brokenness By Joni Jones

He heals the brokenhearted and binds up their wounds ~ Psalm 147:3

I wear a bullseye on my chest, receiving every condemning arrow as if it were the truth leaving me wounded. When others tell me that I am not good enough, through words and actions, I receive them, despite all who I know to be in Jesus. I am full of fear of the critical comments, fear of not measuring up to the standards that I have set for myself. The arrows of critical comments that I have no control over, yet they control me, leave me in a puddle of brokenness, seeking a healer.

Unfortunately, I seek any healer who poses to be one: people's approval, perfection, food, addiction. Yet all these "healers" become more of the problem as they are merely imposters—false and temporary heart fillers which actually empty the soul, instead of filling. A heart in need of healing is vulnerable. It will receive whatever comes its way. Whether it is the lies that fly or the truth that fills, it is ready and primed to receive.

But then He shows up because that is who Jesus is. The Healer of the broken-hearted. The Healer who catches every arrow that comes flying toward His daughter, the one who He calls us His beloved. A bleeding heart needs a Healer who fills every aching hole with His truth about who we are in Him. When Christ's truth overrides the consuming lies, I am found walking in unfamiliar territory. He tells me I am worthy, valuable and am not condemned in Him. It wasn't until I asked Jesus to come and heal my brokenness, that I no longer feared the arrows. I wear His protective coat that guards my heart. At times I do get caught off guard and I am pierced with a dart and crumble under its power. Yet, every time, that is exactly when my Healer comes and does what He does best—loving me back together with His Love, healing my brokenness and binding my wounds. What a good God!

Dear Lord, I praise You for being the Healer of the broken-hearted and for reminding me how valuable I am to You. Thank You for Your protection and Your healing balm that brings comfort to my soul. Amen.

I am Healed

picture

What arrows have pierced your heart and broke it? Where in your past do you need Jesus' healing touch?

ask

How does God's love touch and heal those places in your heart?

pray

What If By Tierney Gill

A man's heart deviseth his way, but the LORD directeth his steps. ~ Proverbs 16:9

George was a tall, athletic man who decided to pursue a career in the Navy. On the enlistment date, he arrived at the docks ready to sail, but his mother pleaded with him to reconsider. Though disappointed at the loss of his opportunity, the teenager submitted to his mother's wishes, sacrificed his personal ambitions, and stayed home. He couldn't have known it then, but this young man would go on to become commander of the Continental Army, leading the ragtag American militia to ultimate victory against the British in the Revolutionary War. His name? General George Washington.

As a history buff, I have been fascinated by this tale of George Washington. What if George had gone ahead with his plans and served in the Royal Navy? Would he have survived to later lead his countrymen or perish in service to Britain's King? The sheer volume of alternate endings to his story and history is mind-boggling.

"What if" is as intellectually stimulating to ask in history as it is in my personal life. I often find myself bogged down in the cycle of endless what if questions. What if I'm not doing what I am supposed to be doing? Or where I am supposed to be?

What if my parents had followed the doctor's advice to not have any more children after the medical complications with my older brother? What if I had gone to school instead of being homeschooled? What if the United States Marines had accepted my attempt to enlist out of high school instead of twice denying me? What if I had stuck with my medical school career track instead of switching to pursue a political path?

The pressure of so many personal decisions can be unbearably paralyzing. But in uncertain times like these, I have found refuge in numerous passages, such as Proverbs 16, which assure me my Lord is there beside me, directing my steps accordingly. Instead of a hair-pulling frustration, each what if becomes a reminder that I am not in control of my life – God is. Perhaps what I think is a detour is Him guiding and leading me towards the future He has for me. I can let the what-ifs go, and trust His guidance and direction step by step, day by day.

Lord, help me rely on You and Your timing, not get bogged down in the what ifs of life and situations outside of my control. I trust and rely on You. Thank You for guiding my steps in this life as I head towards eternity. Amen.

I am Directed by Him

picture

How will you start letting those "what if's" go to trust in God and His timing, guidance, and direction?

ask

What are some of the "what if" questions of your life that seem to still be unanswered?

pray

I am Directed by Him

Roaring Like a Lion By Sue Sherstad

The wicked flee when no man pursues them, but the righteous are bold as a lion.
~ Proverbs 28:1 (AMP)

Timid and bashful I stood there, feeling my face beginning to blush red hot, I just wanted to disappear. I'm shy, you know! Oh God! Help me get through this speech class! I labeled myself "shy," so I couldn't possibly be expected to ever be a speaker—that's just not me. I will always be quiet and timid, or so I thought. After becoming born-again, the Lord showed me in His Word that He didn't create me to be shy; that's a lie of the devil! It took some time to renew my mind, but I gradually understood that my true identity in Christ meant that I had the boldness of a lion in me! Jesus is The Lion of the Tribe of Judah and He is the One living inside of me by His Spirit. He gave me the boldness and courage to preach and teach His Word and I've done so in front of hundreds of people!

You have been made the righteousness of Christ by grace after accepting Jesus as Savior and Lord. His gift of righteousness gives you His authority over the power of the devil. Therefore, as the uncompromisingly righteous sons and daughters of God, we have a boldness that comes with the power of the Holy Spirit to stand against Satan. Resist the spirit of fear and timidity, it is not from God and He didn't make you that way. The Lord has given you the spirit of love, and of power and a sound mind!

When the believers were threatened for preaching the gospel, they prayed. Acts 4:31 says, "And when they had prayed, the place in which they were assembled was shaken; and they were all filled with the Holy Spirit, and they continued to speak the Word of God with freedom and boldness and courage." You can be filled with the Holy Spirit and boldness to face every situation. Don't draw back in cringing fear and give power to Satan. You have an assignment from Jesus that requires boldness and that comes from knowing who you are and remembering you have the greater One living inside you. Arise! Let the Lion of the Tribe of Judah roar back at Satan when he comes pacing around you to intimidate. He is a toothless and defeated foe. Be bold and be strong in the power of His might!

Lord, You are the Lion of the Tribe of Judah living in me! Give me the Boldness of Your Holy Spirit to obey You and fulfill my assignment. Amen!

I am Bold as a Lion

picture

How will you change the way you respond to fear and intimidation?

ask

What did you learn about your identity from this passage?

pray

I am Bold as a Lion

Beloved Daughter By Lisa Danegelis

He brought me to the banqueting house, and His banner over me was love. ~ Song of Sol 2:4 (NKJV)

My journal recounts my desperation as I called out to God in physical, emotional and mental distress. I could not understand why He was not rescuing me from my ongoing desperate situation. "Daddy, let me feel it, let me feel Your comfort and love, don't be silent any longer, speak to me, please, please!"

His response flowed from my pen easily and beautifully:

"I will speak to you of My love. My love does not come neatly packaged in a perfect little box; My love rages and roars. My love is not contained in a setting that is only comfortable and familiar; my love does not only hide and protect, My love proves you. My love is ferocious and bold; my love thrusts the beloved forth into the waves and winds of life so they may know my divine protection, My violent passionate love in the storm. My love pushes, prods and catapults My children forward into unknown territory. It asks for more, demands the best ... it drives My children into fullness; that is My love.

And yet, My love is tender, soft and pure. It is available to all, this magnificent force that never lets go, never lets up, never fails. I am love. All I do is love, all the results are love. Do not despair that you do not see this as love now, you will. ONLY BELIEVE.

My love does not weaken, it strengthens. It is not passive, but productive; it pursues and promotes. My love does not coddle, it cures; it does not worry, it wins. My love waits and watches, it fans the flames and calms the seas. My love is desperate for your whole heart.

I am the Lion of Judah, the Bright and Morning Star, the great I AM. I am in hot pursuit of you, all of you. I am the Purifying Fire, the Healing Balm, and the Deep Cutting Place. I have never promised a seamless, painless life. I have never promised a life abundant outside of an abundant life in Me. The abundance comes in your soul as you know Me, drink Me in, saturate yourself with who I am. When you realize I cannot fail you, you will see all as love. Your life is rich with promise and purpose, rich with My Kingdom. Wait on this love. It leads you. It heals you. It delivers you. You are so loved, My daughter."

Thank You for relentlessly pursuing me with Your love, Father.
Open my eyes to see all as love. Amen.

I am Relentlessly Loved

picture

How can you begin pursuing others in the same love the Father bestows upon us?

ask

God's banner over you and me is love. (Song of Solomon 2:4) What other verses can you think of where God proclaims His great love for you?

pray

I am Relentlessly Loved

Little Foxes By Nilda Campuzano

Catch for us the little foxes, the little foxes that ruin the vineyards, our vineyards that are in bloom.
~ Song of Solomon 2:15

Recently, as I was driving to work, I noticed a small red fox carelessly roaming a very busy intersection. My first reaction was of joy to see such a small, beautiful creature cross my path; my second reaction was of worry, that other drivers might not see him and inadvertently injure him. I prayed and asked God to watch over him and guide him to safety.

Thinking about Mr. Fox, I recalled a Bible verse admonishing us to catch the little foxes that damage the vineyards and I wondered why would anybody be so concerned about those cute creatures. I quickly remembered my grandparents going to great lengths to protect their chickens from the foxes; recalling nights we were awakened because the noisy chickens were alerting everyone of the presence of a fox. My grandparents always told us of the chicken casualties the next day.

Upon further research, I discovered that foxes are also damaging to horticultural enterprises, such as vineyards, because they dig and damage the root system of the vine, eat the fruit, or chew the irrigation systems. As cute as they are, they wreak havoc in the fields. Whether or not we realize it, our lives are vineyards. Every day we take care of our families, our homes, and our communities; each area of our lives representing a vine in our vineyards. Our vines grow and extend, intermingling. When there is fruit in one area, the joy of that fruit is reflected in all areas. Similarly, when there is damage to one area, the effects of that damage can be felt throughout the vineyard. So, how can we protect our life's vineyard from the little foxes?

Before Jesus ascended, He assured the disciples they would not have to face this world alone; that the little foxes would not have the run of our vineyards. He promised to send a Helper—the Holy Spirit is our Helper, giving us power, transforming us into the image of Christ, and guiding us into all truth for every area of our lives. Be encouraged to know that the Holy Spirit within you will guide you—and expose the little foxes that threaten to ruin your blooming vineyard.

Lord, help me to be attentive to the promptings of the Holy Spirit when
He identifies the little foxes that rob me of the blessings you have prepared
for me. Grant me the wisdom and the strength to give my vineyard
the care and nurturing it needs. Amen.

I am Helped

picture

As you examine the different areas of your vineyard, what area would you say needs a special pruning or tender care from our Heavenly Gardener?

ask

Once you identify one area of struggle, ask yourself: what is the little fox I need to catch?

pray

God's Truth Transforms Our Lives By Marlene Dawson

I am my beloved's, and my beloved is mine ~ Song of Solomon 6:3a (NIV)

There was a great song taken from this verse about God's love gently covering us like a flag. Even though I hoped God's love was true, I could not relate at any level. Working to be accepted and loved was all I knew, and I had certainly done nothing to earn the love of God. I tried to win love from people who should have given it freely but did not or could not. When I tried to acquire love, I failed miserably. My husband and I were part of a homegroup through our church, and we decided to study the Song of Solomon in the Bible. Of course, it is the love story of a man and a woman, but it is also an allegory of how wonderfully and intimately God loves each of us. I began seeing God's love as the true love I always needed. I finally understood God wanted a relationship with me because He loves me, not because I finally did enough to earn His love, which I could never do.

We need to learn to grow in our faith and also navigate from our false beliefs to His truth. This is where the Holy Spirit enters the picture: the Bible says He leads us into all truth. As we read the Bible, the Holy Spirit will begin to reveal the error of our thoughts, and if we are lacking wisdom, we can ask God and He will generously give us all we need. "Jesus Loves Me" slowly became a love song as I began believing these words from Song of Solomon 6:3a: "I am my beloved's, and He is mine." Even though I knew these words, I was emotionally disconnected from words on a page. The people in our small group helped me understand and believe that God loved me completely. I began to accept myself, imperfections and all, a process that is taking many years. I also learned that God has given us tools to teach us about Him and His love, then we apply His principles to tell others about His transforming love. Two of the best tools are studying the Bible and spending time in prayer. The Lord wants us to know Him intimately, but He will not force us into a relationship. He always gives us the freedom to choose Him and His ways.

Dear Lord, Please help me to always trust you. Thank You. Amen.

I am His Beloved

picture

How will knowing you are God's beloved change how you look at yourself?

ask

How would you put Song of Solomon 6:3a (NIV) into your own words?

pray

I am His Beloved

I Already AM By Michelle Meade

For unto us a Child is born, unto us a Son is given; and the government shall be upon His shoulder and His Name shall be called Wonderful, Counselor, The Mighty God, The Everlasting Father, The Prince of Peace. ~ Isaiah 9:6 (NKJV)

It was both deftly sobering and profoundly liberating when Holy Spirit whispered, "you've spent your entire life trying to become who you already are." I could sob to reflect on the amount of self-effort generated, expended, and wasted. However, the sob never emerged because of the wave of relief that reverberated through my triune being. I was exhausting myself on the hamster wheel of performance trying to be good enough, prove my value, and grip my boots straps harder to overcome. Imagine the rejoicing that rang through the heavens when I finally agreed with God. The insurmountable weight of my burden backpack was released off my tiny shoulders and placed upon the shoulders of the ONE whom the government shall rest. The Hebrew word for shoulder is "shkem" and means the place of burdens.

When I realized the cost of all my fears and failures had already been paid for, I could twirl and sing. "I ALREADY AM.... I already AM... I already am! I AM Pure, I AM Precious, I AM Powerful!" I don't need to do impossible spiritual gymnastics and land the perfect testimony dismount. I don't need to post 100 "selfies" on Instagram to be seen. And I don't need someone else to validate my story to discover I'm known and loved. I already am.

Here's the secret sauce; to know and believe the love God cherishes for us. "And we know (understand, recognize, are conscious of, by observation and experience) and believe (adhere to, put faith in, and rely on) the love God cherishes for us." 1 John 4:16 sums up the paradigm shift from "Try" to "Trust." Intimately knowing our Wonderful, Counselor, Mighty God, Everlasting Father, and The Prince of Peace, enables us to trust when He says, I already am.

i'm not ashamed of who i am - purchased by the slaughtered Lamb
on The Rock i stand by Grace - all my sins have been erased
when others look i hope they see - Jesus Christ alive in me

Father God, I lay down every fear and doubt that keeps me from Your Arms. Amen.

I am Carefree

picture

What would it look like to twirl and dance in the security of God's Love?

ask

Do you see the invitation to a Father-daughter dance? What is standing in the way of taking His Hand?

pray

I am Carefree

A Friend Forever By Lisa Danegelis

But you, Israel, are My servant, Jacob whom I have chosen, The descendants of Abraham My friend.
. ~ Isaiah 41:8 (NKJV)

My daughter was celebrating the near arrival of her baby girl. This little bundle was unplanned and my daughter unsure, until her words tumbled out: "It turns my stomach to think of giving her up for adoption ... I need her ... she will make my life better." It may sound selfish at first: doesn't a child need a parent, not vice versa? Yet my daughter innately knew this child would be a tremendous blessing in more ways than one.

Did you ever think that God may need us? A friend once told me He does. I had never heard of such a thing! But this seasoned believer knew God as a friend who desired intimacy. She absolutely delighted in Him! Can you envision Him watching you sleep and waiting for you to open your eyes so He can chat with you? So He can smile at you? So He can dance with you throughout your day? If my daughter, in all her "humanness," needs her little one, how much more does our passionate God whose name is Love need His own children? I had the privilege of witnessing my granddaughter's birth. The moment my daughter set her eyes on her little one will forever be embedded in my memory. Absolute joy radiated from her as she said, "That's my baby Mom, mine!" I am convinced the Father rejoices over every one of His children with the same delight!

James 2:23 also tells us that Abraham was called the friend of God. I envision Abraham and God walking along the mountain paths and sitting by the trickling streams. I see them laughing, contemplating and sitting in serene silence. It is interesting that the verse also says, "Abraham believed God." Although we know God is not a respecter of persons, we also know He delights in a heart abandoned to Him. Just as an earthly friendship grows in time through shared experiences, so does our friendship with God. Take His hand as you wander the paths of life. Whisper your secrets and share your fears. Celebrate the joys and let Him wipe your tears. Just as a true friend listens, understands, forgives and loves, so does our faithful God. He is the perfect friend! And don't forget that He may need a listening ear at times too, that's what friends do.....they need each other.

Help me to see myself through Your eyes Father. May I embrace You as not only my Lord and Savior but also my Friend. Amen.

I am Needed

picture

How can you begin to believe you are precious to God?

ask

What is precious to you?

pray

Taking a New Name By Heidi Sampson

This is what the Lord says ... 'Do not fear, for I have redeemed you; I have called you by name, you are mine. ~ Isaiah 43:1 (ESV)

They called me "Ms. Heidi" as they always do. I have gone by that name for over 60 kids in foster care. Yet in the middle of another chaotic day, when my children purposefully didn't call me 'Mom', it felt like a stab in my heart. I am following a call directly from the Lord to mother children who need it. Not being called "Mom" comes with the territory. Most of my kids have living parents, they just need a safe home for the time being. It seems to be no big deal when kids don't use the title of "mom" for me. Yet, when I lose track of who I am in Christ, it is easy to become bitter. I allow myself to listen to the lies from the depths of hell that *I am no longer worth it when my kids fail to recognize me with a title I think I deserve. I tell myself that I put the work into raising them. I love them without conditions. I teach instead of punish. I am the one up all night with their fears. I am the one that feeds and rocks and sings and cleans for them.* But she still gets to be called "mom". Fostering and adopting does not feel victorious on days like this. It feels lonely as if I am fighting a battle with no end. It feels like I am giving up my life to fix someone else's mistake.

God so gently reminds me through kind words from a friend or through the encouragement of my husband that it is not about me. This is not my fight. It does not matter what they call me. HIS name is Victory. I am not doing all this just to earn a name for myself. No label or certificate will give me worth because God has redeemed me. God has called me by name and tells me that I am His. And He does this for you too. I continue to press on proudly as 'Ms. Heidi' because the Almighty God has given me a new name. Call to mind God's redemption of your story today whether anyone else can see it or not. God does not call us to a life full of victory, but of faithfulness to Him.

Lord, help me to take my eyes off of my own accomplishments. Show me that You have called me. Forgive me for failing to recognize Your voice. Help me to live in the power of Your redemption. Amen.

I am Called by My Name

picture

Imagine what your life would be if all titles were taken away from you. Would you be confident solely in the name that Christ has given you?

ask

What title have you found security in? Is there an identity that you hold too tightly?

pray

Rebuilding By Heidi Sampson

You are My witnesses,' declares the LORD, 'And My servant whom I have chosen, so that you may know and believe Me. ~ Isaiah 43:10a (NASB)

At 15 years old, my identity was found in athletics and academics. I had natural abilities in leadership and loved overachieving. That was until I was diagnosed with Type 1 Diabetes. I woke up with symptoms that suddenly made it difficult to get out of bed. As an active, healthy teenager, this was concerning, and my parents took me to the doctor immediately. And that's when it happened. The vision I had for my future was stripped away. I was admitted to the hospital as doctors gave me medication and educated me on how to care for myself. That day in November took my feet out from under me. I had once been self-reliant and independent, but suddenly I saw weakness, dependency, and limits as huge mountains ahead of me.

Everything I knew felt unstable. God was rebuilding my identity and my future in Him, and it hurt. In the midst of the physical and mental turmoil I was experiencing, a mentor called me. As soon as I picked up the phone she began to sing, "Rise and shine and give God the glory, glory". I was brought to tears as God spoke to my heart through those words. This dear friend knew exactly what my heart needed to remember: who I was before and after Type 1 Diabetes was irrelevant compared to my identity as a child of God. In the days and weeks following my diagnosis, I heard doctors talk about scary things that would alter my life forever. It was challenging and physically painful at times to remember who God made me to be in the midst of giving myself injections and grasping my new responsibilities.

Although Diabetes was a complete surprise for me and my family, it was not unexpected to God. I often recalled the words of that song from my friend to wake up each day and give God glory. As my life was reconstructed after Type 1 Diabetes, there was a comfort in knowing that my Creator formed me and set me apart for Himself. Hope was born within me as I remembered God designed my body, however sick, to bring Him glory. Chronic illness could not define me, I am a child of God.

Lord, help me to "rise and shine" for You today. Thank you for creating me to bring You glory. Amen.

I am being Rebuilt

picture

Write down 3 ways that you can glorify God in uncertainty. Remember He has chosen you!

ask

Do things feel unstable in your life? How is God using that to rebuild your identity?

pray

I am being Rebuilt

The Old Has Gone; The New is Here! By Noreen Lessmann

Remember not the former things, nor consider the things of old. Behold, I am doing a new thing; now it springs forth, do you not perceive it? I will make a way in the wilderness and rivers in the desert
~ Isaiah 43:18 -19 ESV

Spring is here! A spring snowfall in Wisconsin glistens upon the trees. The air is clean, fresh and crisp. Ice is crackling upon the lake shores. The sun is glistening upon the snow-covered trees. It is so beautiful. Spring is a new beginning. Like spring, our identity in Christ simulates a new beginning. We are awakening to new growth, like tree buds upon the trees. The old is gone the new is here. Do not dwell on, fret over and ponder the old things , things in the past. Acknowledge them and let them pass. God is doing a new thing in your life. God will make a new way for you.

God gives us a "re-do." Ever need a "re-do"? I have screwed up on countless occasions—done things I should not have done; said things left better unsaid; made the wrong choices. I've certainly needed and welcomed a "re-do." Our God gives us a new beginning and the old is gone. Because of this new life, It just doesn't matter what sins we've committed; what we've said or done. God forgives us. In response, we need to forgive ourselves. The old is gone and the new is here. In Christ, we can release the weight that burdens us and we can release struggles and strongholds that hinder our progress. The old is gone. The new is here. In Christ, we are a new creation. Now it springs forth.

Dear Lord, please help me to relinquish the past that detains my progress in living out my true identity in You. Amen.

I am Made New

picture

What could happen if Christ's strength was within you? How would things be different if you allowed God to complete this task through you?

ask

Is there a task or circumstance in your life that seems impossible to complete?

pray

Do Not Forget By Kimberly Krueger

Remember the former things long past, for I am God, and there is no other; I am God, and there is no one like Me. ~ Isaiah 46:9 (NASB)

It was almost Christmas and there wasn't any food to serve. I was short on all the staples and Christmas gifts, too. As a single mom with eleven mouths to feed, I knew what that meant: I'd have to take another dreaded trip to the local food pantry with hopes they'd be giving away more than hams. By this point in my walk with God, I knew in my knower that "food pantry client" was NOT my real identity. So, I straightened my crown and got in the car, but I couldn't shake the dichotomy. My mind kept trying to reconcile who God said I was with these meager circumstances. After years of believing His Word, my spirit KNEW that I was blessed and favored—a daughter of the King! But another humbling trip to the food pantry made my mind and emotions painfully aware that after waiting many years to see this identity manifest fully, I would have to wait some more. As I walked toward the building, I surrendered to discouragement.

Suddenly, beautiful, large snowflakes began to cascade all around me. While marveling at the sight, a still, small voice spoke to my heart. "This is the last time you will ever need to go to a food pantry. Rejoice in that, My daughter, but do not ever forget what this feels like." Wow! "Do not forget" resonated through my being like an echo in a canyon. The purity and tenderness of God's message covered me like those majestic snowflakes. Suddenly, I could clearly envision my future-self encouraging other women with stories of my "food pantry days," and the transformation in my life that would follow. I saw that in order for my future self to be a true source of hope, I needed to first experience the struggle that takes place when our circumstances totally contradict the new identity we've embraced by faith.

There are reasons I would love to forget my food pantry days, but I will not. He was faithful there! And now, on the other side, I get to marvel at how He transformed a single-mother-welfare-recipient who believed she was a daughter of the King, into a successful business owner and mouthpiece for Him. For His glory, I will not forget! I will remember the former things as I shout from the rooftops, "There is no one like my God!

Lord, there is no one like You! I will remember what You brought me out of and how You've made everything new so I can strengthen and encourage others. Amen.

I am Brought Out

picture

Picture a time when your circumstances contradicted your God-given identity. Describe it.

ask

Ask yourself if that experience strengthened your faith? Why or why not?

pray

When Life is Messy, I Know Whose I Am By Eleanor Weldie

But the Lord GOD helps me; therefore I have not been disgraced; therefore I have set my face like a flint, and I know that I shall not be put to shame. ~ Isaiah 50:7 (NIV)

Can I be honest for a second? I think it's really ironic that I'm currently writing a devotional for a book on identity. See, my life is kind of messing with my identity right now. I am 22, graduated from college early, resigned from a job I was forcing myself to take, unaware of any plans God has for me, living back home, and just generally unsure about who I am or where I'm going.

In high school, identity is relatively easy. You define yourself based on who you sit with at the lunch table: jocks, preps, nerds. In college, your identity revolves around your major, which bands you listen to, and for which campus organization you're in leadership. It's harder now, and not knowing it brings shame. College graduates are expected to have a well-defined goal, a career in their back pocket, maybe a steady romantic relationship, and definitely a plan. When you have none of that, what is your identity? Who are you? And the harder questions: How could you let yourself get to this point? Weren't you supposed to have spent the last four years figuring yourself out? How much longer do you need? So, yeah, I don't really know my identity right now. I'm figuring that out even as I sit here and type, trying to get the words out.

There's one thing I do know. One thing I must refuse to forget, even when I can't bring myself to proclaim it: I am God's. That's my identity. When I am tempted to believe the lies of this world and the lies of the enemy and the lies in my own head, I need to be reminded of who God says I am.

I am an overcomer. *I am clean.*
I am a beloved daughter. *I am good.*
I am an heiress. *I am loved.*
I am alive. *I am His!*

That's when the shame falls away. It is in these truths I can rest, and my soul is reminded that the Lord GOD helps me. I have not been disgraced. I can say confidently, I am God's.

God, even when I don't know who I am, You know.
Banish the shame of the world from my life, and let me focus
only on who You say I am. Amen.

I am God's

picture

What causes you to feel shame? How do the Words God speaks over you cover that shame?

ask

What is a list of some of the identities God has given you?

pray

By His Stripes By Kimberly Krueger

The chastisement for our peace was upon Him, And by His stripes we are healed.
~ Isaiah 53:5b (NKJV)

Have you ever asked the Lord questions like: 'Lord, will my family ever be healed of all our hurts?' 'Lord, will my health ever be restored?' 'Lord, will I ever not struggle with eating my feelings?' 'Lord, will my broken heart ever be whole?' I used to ask Him these kinds of questions all the time. I would read verses in the Bible like "who the Son sets free is free indeed," (John 8:36) and "It was for freedom that Christ set us free," (Galatians 5:1) and I would think, Hmm. I don't feel very free. I couldn't reconcile all the talk of freedom with my life that was riddled with so much brokenness.

And then I studied Isaiah 53. It was a game-changer! Isaiah 53 is a prophetic description of the death of our Savior. His piercing, scourging and nail-scarred body were written about thousands of years before He was even born. That is amazing in and of itself, but what is even more amazing is what these few verses in the Bible really mean for us. My eyes were completely opened to the fact that Jesus' scourging, piercing, and death on the Cross are the cure for every single thing that ails mankind. Every. Single. Thing. He left nothing out. One power-packed example is found in verse 5: "By His stripes, we are healed," literally means by His stripes, we are mended. In other words, He was torn apart so we could be sewn together. That is how far He went to answer our "Will we ever" questions. His answer is clearly YES!

Friend, His flesh was torn away from His body, so He could sew up and permanently mend your broken heart, family, health, finances, mind, and relationships. 'By His stripes' have become some of my favorite words in the whole Bible. I take no pleasure in what He suffered, but I'll tell you what ... I won't let it be wasted on me! I will believe and receive this expensive promise! Will you believe that His stripes were His YES to mending you?

Jesus, what You did for me ... there are no words. Thank You, from the bottom of my heart, for being torn apart so that I could be sewn back together. I know it is Your truth and love that mends me in every way, even today. Thank You that by Your stripes, I am healed. Amen.

I am Healed

picture

Imagine Jesus receiving those stripes with you in mind. Did He go to such lengths to leave you unmended? Why or why not?

ask

What are the broken things you need Jesus to sew together in your life today? Make a list here and then write a prayer asking Him to do so below.

pray

I am Healed

Invited to the Party By Eleanor Weldie

Come, everyone who thirsts, come to the waters; and he who has no money, come, buy and eat!
Come, buy wine and milk without money and without price....Listen diligently to me, and eat what is
good, and delight yourselves in rich food. Incline your ear, and come to me; hear, that your soul may
live, and I will make you an everlasting covenant, my steadfast, sure love for David.
~ Isaiah 55:1-2b-3 (ESV)

I still remember the feeling of shock coursing through my body as I sat on my bed that Friday after school. It had been a good day. I felt like I was building new friendships with some girls; I even aced my Biology quiz. But as we were waiting to be picked up from school in the sweltering South Carolina heat, a winter-like chill settled over me when I heard, "Yeah, you're actually not invited to my birthday party." I couldn't believe it. It was her sweet sixteenth birthday and it was going to be the coolest party of the semester—and she told me in front of all my classmates that I wasn't invited!

When we experience blatant rejection, it's crushing. Looking back, a sixteenth birthday party with skating and ice cream definitely wasn't an event I just had to be at, but the feeling of not being invited took me a while to get over. When I read Isaiah 55, I am reminded that uninvited and unwanted is NOT my identity. Instead, my Father calls to me: "Come!" He has prepared a rich spread of delightful foods before me. He knows this will be the coolest party not only of the semester but of a lifetime. He wants to gather people to Him, to feast together, to give good gifts for free, to offer life. My Father doesn't turn anyone away. The only admission fee is to be thirsty, to have no money, to listen to His words.

The shock and sting of being uninvited in this world are hurtful. But there is a place you and I can run to when we are met with this sting: it is the life God alone provides. He promises His covenant - His steadfast, sure love that leads to life. This love will never treat you like you're not worthy or push you away. This love looks at you gently and beacons, "Come! Come to the table! I want you here! I want you to receive good things."

Father, forgive me for the times I fail to believe You have invited me to Your table and the times I let my emotions or experiences in this broken world stop me from going to Your feast. Give me the strength to accept the invitation with nothing to bring but my thirst for You. Thank You that You offer something more substantial than food – the Bread of Life that gives me joy and peace and life to the fullest in You. Amen.

I am Invited

picture

How do you feel when you are invited as you are, no questions asked? How can you start inviting people into your own life as Jesus has invited you?

ask

In Mark 2:13-15, Jesus calls Levi, a tax collector, to follow him and later ends up reclining at his table with "many tax collectors and sinners" (Mark 2:15, ESV). Why does Jesus often gather people to Him around the table? What is the significance of tax collectors and sinners gathering with him?

pray

I am Invited

Shame By Noreen Lessmann

I remember as a child feeling a sense of shame. In comparison with the other kids, I did not have a nice bike. As a matter of fact, it was a bike pieced together from mismatched parts. The kids in grade school made fun of my bike and I was embarrassed. I should have been grateful just to have a bike. I made do with this mismatched bike put together with various pieces and it got me from point A to point B in my Chicago neighborhood. When I finally graduated to a nice bike, I was on top of the world. You would have thought I won the lottery. Oh, man, I made it. I had a purple bike with three speeds. So cool! I would speed all over on that bike, carefree, wind blowing in my hair, and be home when the street lights came on.

God is like the benefactor of that bike. Instead of shame and disgrace, He provides double honor, double blessings for all your trouble. God replaces the miserable feelings of shame, humiliation, and embarrassment with a healthy identity in Christ, just like I traded in my old bike. We can rejoice in our inheritance knowing God is our source, but we have to be willing to make the trade. It's time to upgrade that old bike!

Oh, Lord allow me to have a glimpse of the mirror image that You see
n me. Thank You for Your promises of a double portion and more than
enough. Thank you for an inheritance and everlasting joy. Praise you, Lord.
I stand in joyful anticipation of your blessing and your promises.
Thank you for the dreams that you tuck away in my heart and the
everlasting joy that you provide. Amen.

I am Unashamed

picture

How does Christ see you? How can you live your life seeing yourself as Christ sees you?

ask

In what areas of your life do you experience a sense of shame or embarrassment? Does Christ see any shame or embarrassment when he looks at you?

pray

I am Unashamed

He Calls Me Delightful By Nilda Campuzano

No more shall men call you Forsaken or your land Desolate; you will be called by a new name that the mouth of the Lord shall bestow ... you will be called My Delight ... ~ Isaiah 62:2, 4 (NIV)

A few years back I worked as a server at a restaurant. I remember a particular couple I used to serve because we always had meaningful conversations; they were eager to learn all about me and they always left me feeling energized and cared for, even though I was the one serving them. One day, one of them stopped me as I was thanking them for coming. He gently put his hand on my shoulder, looked at me with kindness and flashed a sincere smile while saying, "Darling, you are simply delightful." My knees buckled, and my eyes got all teary while I sheepishly replied: "Awww ... I've been called a lot of things, but I have never been called delightful."

He continued looking deeply into my eyes and said, "Well, I'm surprised, because you are." I hugged him and spent the rest of my shift walking on cloud nine. He found me delightful.

Many moons have passed since then, and many storms have come my way. I have gone through a divorce, loneliness, heartbreak, isolation, depression, shame, constant fear, as well as periods of happiness and joy, a newfound love, and new beginnings. Regret has overcome me at times, as I look at my life and my age and feel that despite all my efforts and hard work, I have very little to show for all the years I've been given. Then today, as I listened to an audio devotional, I was taken aback by this verse:

"No more shall men call you Forsaken or your land Desolate; you will be called by a new Name that the mouth of the Lord shall bestow; you will be called My Delight."

I am His delight. He calls me delightful! My memory raced back to my friend at the restaurant and I was filled with all the emotion that comes when someone finds you delightful. My heart felt joy, peace, and a deep sense of belonging; I felt seen, acknowledged, secure. My Heavenly Father calls me delightful! The world and life itself can be cruel; maybe you have been or are being called all sorts of not-so-nice names. Today I want to remind you that it is not what you are called that matters, but what you answer to. And you get to answer to "delightful."

Heavenly Father, Your Word tells me that You call me by a new name. Please reveal that name to me and give me the grace to walk securely in my identity. Amen.

I am Delightful

picture

The Bible tells us that God calls us by name; what is the name God uses to address you when He talks to you?

ask

Are the names you call yourself congruent with the names God calls you?

pray

I am Delightful

Life In the Potter's Hand By Lisa Danegelis

But now, O Lord, You are our Father; we are the clay, You our potter; and we are the work of Your hand.
~ Isaiah 64:8 (NKJV)

I am a professional baker. I envision a product and begin. The Piece De Resistance can be many things: a buttery cake, a rustic bread or a creamy mousse. The time between the mixing bowl and cooling rack is called "process." Just as I take a melange of raw ingredients and create, God tells us to bring what we have to Him, however seemingly insignificant, however broken, promising to make something amazing.

Yesterday, I was asking a thoughtful young man about whether he was ready to accept Jesus as his Savior. He indicated he didn't feel worthy, as if he had to clean up his life first. I explained the restoration work is done by God after we come to Him. We do the surrendering, God does the changing. Just as I knead, shape and proof my bread dough, so the Potter takes us, a piece of unformed clay, and creates beauty.

As I was musing over these things, God spoke: "Oh my precious girl, the surrendered heart is such a blessing to Me. I can mold, shape, and take my time to create such a work of art! All the great art pieces throughout the centuries were crafted with deep thoughtfulness, time, and care. Too much time some thought, as they waited for the master's hand to finish. A work of art from the heart is created with passion; not for money or even applause, but to fulfill the master's longings and depth of expression, to bring awe to others as it goes on to feed their souls as well. I delight in creating masterpieces!"

Pottery can be as small as a tiny trinket or as massive as the world's largest vase, weighing 650 pounds! The designs, textures, and colors are endless! Sounds a bit like the human race, doesn't it? I believe God used the pottery analogy for this reason! Striking though, when pottery is shattered, it can be re-created into something even more beautiful - mosaics! Maybe you fell off the Potter's wheel or jumped off yourself. Or, maybe you don't feel worthy enough to get on at all like my young friend. Surrender your broken parts into the Master's loving hands—magnificent restoration awaits!

"It may be unfulfilled, it may be unrestored, but anything laid before the Lord will not be unredeemed." -Anonymous.

I know Your Potter's wheel is gentle and loving, Father; I surrender the broken pieces of my life into Your hands and wait as You create beauty. Amen.

I am Clay in His Hands

picture

What does your ideal life look like? How does it feel to know God can take your broken pieces and make them an ideal masterpiece? Are you willing to surrender to His hand that wishes goodness and beauty upon you?

ask

Listen to this quote by an anonymous source: "It may be unfulfilled, it may be unrestored, but anything laid before the Lord will not be unredeemed." How is the Lord redeeming you and shaping you today?

pray

I am Clay in His Hands

Your Life is No Accident By Susan Tyler

The word of the Lord came to me, saying, before I formed you in the womb, I knew you before you were born, I set you apart. ~ Jeremiah 1:4-5 (NIV)

I am so in awe of God and the love that He has for us. We mean so much to Him that he designed a purpose for each of our lives before we ever were created. Can you grasp the significance of this truth from Jeremiah? Before God informed Jeremiah of his calling, he pulled him aside and revealed that He had prearranged for Jeremiah to be a Prophet before his parents had conceived him—he was created (in part) to prophesy over Judah and Jerusalem.

You were set apart for a purpose.

Regardless of the situation surrounding your birth, what you have thought or what you have been told, your life is not an accident! You have a purpose in God's vision that only you can fulfill. The Bible says, "All the days planned for me were written in your book before I was one day old." (Psalm 139:16 NCV). Ephesians 2:10 declares, "For we are God's masterpiece. He has created us anew in Christ Jesus, so we can do the good things he planned for us long ago."

There is no one like you on earth because no one else has your exact DNA and distinct blend of skill sets. God wired you with certain ambitions, desires, and drives for His use in expanding His Kingdom. I have been spending much time thinking about this topic as I enter my mid-50s. I ask myself, "Am I doing all that God created me to do?" When I get to Heaven, I want to hear God say, "Well done, Susan." I am on a quest to live out my purpose with confidence and boldness. What about you?

Lord, I feel the love that You have for me, and I thank You for the privilege of serving You. Help me to know and embrace my calling with humility and confidence, knowing that You have sent me and will go before me just as You promised that You would. In Jesus' Name I pray, Amen.

I am Set Apart

picture

Picture yourself doing what you do best. What are the gifts, passions, and desires that God has wired you with?

ask

Describe how God might want you to use those gifts, passions, and desires to further His kingdom.

pray

Appointed By Nilda Campuzano

Then the Lord stretched out His hand and touched my mouth, and the Lord said to me ... See, I have appointed you this day ... To pluck up and to break down, To destroy and to overthrow, To build and to plant. ~ Jeremiah 1:9-10 (NASB)

Recently, my son and I had a very interesting conversation regarding name brands and value. For as long as I could, I got away buying his clothes at thrift shops. Considering kids outgrow their clothes faster than you can do laundry, spending money on brand names didn't make financial sense to me. The jig was up once my oldest hit middle school; at that time, wearing a certain brand and developing a sense of style became important to him.

The conversation about name brands took me to other types of labels: the ones we use to describe ourselves. It turns out, as much as I despise labels, I discovered I had imposed many damaging labels on myself. I have moved through my life wearing those labels; allowing them to define and limit me.

At an early age, I called myself unloved, rejected, abandoned. Later I added unworthy, used up, ashamed. After a few years, I took on broken, alone, insecure, lost. The results of walking through life wearing those labels have been devastating. I allowed the enemy to fill me with lies about my value and my worth. But long ago, I knew there was a strong calling in my life. I knew early in life that God had a plan for me, and that He wanted to use my life to bring healing and restoration to many. Sadly, through many bad decisions and experiences, I came to believe that God had rescinded His vision for my life and that I had successfully derailed all His plans with each fall and failure.

I was glad to discover I am not that powerful; I don't have the power to derail God's plan for me. He appointed me, He anointed me and consecrated me. The Bible says all our days are written in His book, so He knew I would lose my way, yet He still called me by name and planted a seed in my heart that would bear fruit in its time. Knowing this gave me the courage to tear down every label I ever attached to myself; I stripped each one of those labels until I got to the only one that matters: appointed.

Dear God, the world fills us daily with messages of unworthiness and our weaknesses. But your Word tells us that we were chosen and appointed before we were formed in our mother's womb. Give us the strength we need to boldly step into what you created us to be. Amen.

I am Appointed

picture

What are the words do you most often use to describe yourself?

ask

Based on what you know about yourself, what is one area God has appointed you to conquer in His Name?

pray

I am Appointed

I Was Created for a Purpose By Susan Tyler

For I know the plans I have for you, declares the Lord, plans to prosper you and not to harm you, plans to give you hope and a future. ~ Jeremiah 29:11 (NIV)

A few years ago, I felt deep inside my belly that God had a greater plan for my life than what I was experiencing. God literally changed my life overnight when I accepted a job opportunity that required me to move to another state. I was self-employed before the move. I loved the freedom that came with running my own business, yet something was missing. I knew I was created for a higher calling.

When yearning for more, I prayed to God asking for direction. Shortly afterward, He answered my prayers when one of my clients presented me with a job offer at his company. It was a God-sized offer, so in my early 50s, I decided to reinvent myself and move to the Jersey Shore. The best part about the move is that I am now pursuing my calling to help leaders further develop their skills and discover their purpose in helping to advance God's Kingdom on earth.

God has wired you with a unique mixture of spiritual gifts, passions, abilities, and personality. You were designed to play a role in history—in expanding His Kingdom. It is an assignment that only you can complete. It is your destiny—not your mother's, not your father's, not your husband's, or even your pastor's destiny; it is yours!

However, here is the painful truth: You can go through your entire life and miss God's purpose for your life—if you are afraid to step out. Getting to your destiny will require hard work and for you to step out into the unknown without being able to predict the outcome. But you can have confidence in the fact that Our God, the Good Shepherd, will guide you. He wants you to succeed. You make the first move, believe, and hold Him to His promises! He is a Keeper of His Word. He will do it for you just as He has done it for me, time and time again!

Dearest Father, I thank You that You have designed a great plan and purpose for the woman who is reading this now. Speak to her, Lord, and show her the direction in which she is to move. Guide her, Lord, just as You promised that You would. In Jesus' Name I pray, Amen.

I am Full of Purpose

picture

Picture Jesus looking you in the eye and speaking Jeremiah 29:11 directly to you. Write your response here.

ask

Can you identify with my story? What part of your purpose might you be avoiding now because of fear, a lack of funds, or other existing responsibilities?

pray

I am Full of Purpose

In Over My Head By Heidi Sampson

He said to me, 'Son of man, stand up on your feet and I will speak to you.' As He spoke, the Spirit came into me and raised me to my feet, and I heard Him speaking to me. ~ Ezekiel 2:1-2 (NIV)

After two years of marriage, God moved my husband, Jonathon, and I from Michigan to South Carolina to work in a residential group home. Soon after we began, Jonathon was playing outside with some of the kids. Suddenly, he came inside with hives on his legs. Having no allergies, Jonathon was confused by what caused this. I went to get medicine. Before I could get back, hives spread over his whole body and into his mouth. I immediately contacted a coworker next door, and he drove Jonathon to the hospital. Things happened quickly, and panic set in as I realized I was left with nine lively boys! I was overwhelmed as I served an ill-constructed dinner, gathered kids to shower, and completed a chaotic bedtime routine. I felt desperate to hear an update from the hospital. Eventually, Jonathon came home feeling better, but with no answers as to why this happened. I was overwhelmed at what we had experienced, yet thankful God enabled us to survive the day. Fast forward 12 hours and the exact same scenario occurred, except this time the reaction was more extreme. I was afraid. Again, a coworker quickly drove him to the hospital, and I was caught alone and in chaos. I barely made it through the previous night. How could I do this all again? Everyone survived, and since then, we have learned Jonathon is severely allergic to fire ant bites.

This passage in Ezekiel parallels those days of distress. God gave the command for Ezekiel to stand, but then proceeded to stand him up! God said, "Do this. Here, let me do it with you." That is what it looks like to have an identity in Christ. When God asks for obedience, I always assume God wants me, in my own strength, to obey. God told Ezekiel what to do, and then He came and completed it! This is a fantastic picture of how God enables us with His identity. I could feel God completing the tasks before me in those tense days. He was stretching my faith and trust in His plan, all while giving me His name. Sometimes finding yourself in Christ is proclaiming who He made you to be, but oftentimes, it means complete dependence on His strength.

Jesus, thank you for equipping me by putting
Your strength within me. Amen.

I am Lifted by Him

picture

What could happen if Christ's strength was within you? How would things be different if you allowed God to complete this task through you?

ask

Is there a task or circumstance in your life that seems impossible to complete?

pray

I am Lifted by Him

Loving Mercy By Heidi Sampson

Act justly ... love mercy ... walk humbly with your God. ~ Micah 6:8 (NIV)

My husband and I went to the court hearing that removed the rights of our boys' biological parents. Selfishly, I went to see the awful people who mistreated my children. Yet after court began, I found myself in tears listening to these parents speak. But he has done so many bad things. I am dealing with the repercussions of his choices, I told myself as my heart broke. Abuse and neglect were never part of their parenting plan. Life happened, and they found themselves drowning in bad decisions. As I left the court that day, I was frustrated and conflicted. Jesus, this would be much easier if I did not care. But I do care. God desires mercy from me.

What does mercy have to do with finding my identity in Christ? I have been wrestling with this question as I find my purpose in marriage, parenting, and foster care. God has been teaching me there is only one way to give His mercy to others, and that is to be secure in who God declares I am. Being tender-hearted and compassionate to the people around me is difficult to do when I am insecure. I have to be 100% confident of my worth and who holds my future in order to give sacrificially of myself. After caring for precious children in foster care who have been treated unfairly, I do not want to speak positively about their biological family. If given an opportunity, I do not want to meet them at a visit. I let the caseworker do that. But that is the easy thing to do.

Christ gave His whole life and purpose to serving and saving others, to make them feel His love. It becomes my job to continue His work in giving everything I am to do the same. I have to take on God's identity by becoming His child and embracing that I was created in His perfect image, to reflect Him. Our God is a merciful God. What is Mercy? It is showing leniency, compassion, or forgiveness when judgment or punishment is deserved. My actions are a direct reflection of my Creator, so I must be merciful. God has made me to have a soft heart for His people like He has given you. I can only be truly merciful to others when I know God's opinion is the only one that matters, and when I am living in who I was created to be

Jesus, open my eyes to places of insecurity within myself. I humble myself before You. Thank you for creating me with a tender heart like Yours. Show me who needs Your mercy from me today. Amen.

I am Humble

picture

Read God's promises aloud. Let them strengthen who you are because of the security you have in Christ.

ask

What is preventing me from being merciful to others? Who do I need to be forgiving toward?

pray

Hind's Feet By Sue Sherstad

The Lord is my Strength, my personal bravery, and my invincible army; He makes my feet like hind's feet and will make me to walk [not stand still in terror, but to walk] and make spiritual progress upon my high places [of trouble, suffering, or responsibility]. ~ Habakkuk 3:19 (AMP)

In times of great trial and suffering, we can find strength in the midst of chaos and uncertainty. The Prophet Habakkuk found himself in distressing circumstances when Judah fell away from God into idolatry and evil. He put his hope in the Lord and compared the strength he received to that of hind's feet.

A hind is a female deer that can place her back feet exactly where her front feet stepped. She can run securely and with precision in times of danger and escape predators! This enables her to navigate difficult and rocky terrain to climb high places away from her enemy. This scripture has special meaning to me personally. It was declared over me by my pastor at a very dark time in my life when I was desperate for any kind of hope. He said, "The Lord is making your feet like hind's feet, to walk on your troubled places." This is meaningful because the Lord equipped me to run with "spiritual hind's feet." The result of a date rape put me in bondage to ten years of panic attacks and the torment of paralyzing fear at night. I grabbed ahold of the spiritual truth in this verse to rise up and overcome my circumstances.

As I grew in the Lord, the revelation came of my identity in Christ, and I made spiritual progress to defeat fear in my life. His perfect love promises to cast out all fear! This truth became alive to me and I put my trust in His love. I took to heart Ephesians 6:10 – "Be strong in the Lord, draw your strength from Him." The Lord became my strength and personal bravery to face the enemy with boldness. He is my invincible army standing with me, for greater is He who is in me than he that is in the world. Using praise and the Word of God as my mighty weapons of warfare, the stronghold of fear crumbled! I made the choice to not stand still in terror, but to arise in the power and authority given me as a child of God.

Heavenly Father, I put my hope and trust in You. Make my feet like hind's feet to walk victoriously on my high places of trouble and suffering. I will not stand still in terror, but give me Your strength making me brave to move forward in faith! In Jesus Name! Amen.

I am Brave

picture

What can you overcome learning to run with Hind's Feet?

ask

What did you learn about Hind's Feet?

pray

Free to Be Me By Joni Jones

The Lord your God is with you, He is mighty to save. He will take great delight in you, He will quiet you with His love, He will rejoice over you with singing. ~ Zephaniah 3:17 NIV 1984

God was always in my story, weaving it together, even though I didn't know Him. It was at my lowest point in life, as on a quest to find myself, that I lost myself. Who am I besides unlovable? Nowhere else to go, I looked up. The day I cried out to God, I felt lifted out of the quicksand that had been sucking me further away from who I was born to be, but deeper into who I thought I should be. God met me right where I was with an explosive love that I have never experienced before. It was as if He whispered straight into my heart, "I love you. Come to Me as you are so I can transform you into who you were born to be: perfectly loved by Me. Walk with Me and I will show you how to live as one beloved by Me. I have created you. You are My workmanship. Now, will you receive all you were born to be? All Mine!" Life-changing words that became truth to me the moment I looked up.

So I reached up and took hold of the One whose hand was reaching down to me in the pit. I didn't have to clean up my act, because He pursued me just as I was. He wiped off the dirt, the hurt, and the lies and the pain with His blood that set me free. The day I looked up, He had His eyes on me. God seeks us in our lostness and searching, as He is with us, delighting in who He created us to be. We are His beautiful masterpieces whom He rejoices over with singing. So, why not dance and sing as one who is so loved by the Creator?

God rejoices over us, just because that is His delight. When His love pierces your heart, you'll want to sing and dance and shout for joy. God sees us, not as we see ourselves. He sees His precious children in whom He is so pleased that all He wants to do is love. The One who matters says you matter and that is all that matters.

Lord, I can hardly believe You delight in me. Help me to believe that You have created me perfectly. I want to dance and shout in the freedom that comes from being Your child. Thank You for making that possible. Amen.

I am Free to be Me

picture

How can you dance and sing as one loved by God as you are in the process of becoming all who He is making you to be?

ask

How does the truth that you don't have to clean up your act in order to come to the Lord make you feel?

pray

I am Free to be Me

The Smallest Steps By Heidi Sampson

Do not despise these small beginnings, for the Lord rejoices to see the work begin...
~ Zechariah 4:10a (NLT)

In the past, neglect was not seen as traumatic to a child. We now know that a child who has been neglected, has been consistently told, every time they are ignored, they do not exist. The reason my adopted kids have trouble functioning is because they do not think they have or deserve life. It saddens me to say, but this means, the 'after' picture of our kids' adoption looks eerily similar to the 'before'. The only distinction is when our kids yell, "You are NOT my mom and dad," we can now assure them we are.

Tragically, that makes no difference to them. They feel the pain of rejection with every breath. My children act how they do because no adult has shown them they are living, breathing people. There are various questions the boys will ask, but one specifically defines the extent they have been neglected. "If we saw our first mom and dad, would they remember us?" It is heartbreaking to hear their self-doubt. As parents, it is imperative we notice their behaviors—good and bad. My kids heal by hearing their new, adopted names in court, and when we explain once more we will not give up on them. Addressing their existence is a meager portion of the work in adoption.

The adoption of my children is a mirror of the adoption I have received as a believer. How many times do I fail to remember whose child I am? How many times does God have to remind me that He notices me—the good and bad; and that I was given a new identity as His child? In adoption, a child is not expected to instantly change after the paperwork is completed. Joining a family is hard work! Healing must occur before a child can fully step into his new identity. God is not asking us for immediate, drastic change. He wants to see the transformation of our hearts as we grow. When I get frustrated at my kids for acting out of fear instead of the security they now hold, I remember my own actions as a daughter of the King. God celebrates my 'small beginnings' because He is not expecting instant perfection. Following Jesus is a marathon, not a sprint! Accept God's grace as you take on the new identity He has given you.

God, may I see Your reminders today of how loved I am? Help me to start the work to become securely attached to You. Thank you for noticing even the smallest step toward finding myself in You. Amen.

I am a work in Progress

picture

Write down Jude 1:22 and place it somewhere prominent. Remind yourself to accept God's grace today in your efforts to serve Him.

ask

What areas of life are you expecting instant change or perfection from yourself? Is there something you have yet to begin due to a fear you won't master it?

pray

I am a work in progress

The Say-So of God By Michelle Meade

But He answered and said, "It is written, 'Man shall not live by bread alone, but by every word that proceeds from the mouth of God." ~ Matthew 4:4 (NKJV)

God must teach us that His Word trumps every other perceived reality; that His "say-so" is 100% reliable. This belief, like any other, will be proven through testing. I began to understand this concept through a seven-day fast while preparing and serving delicious food to my family. Agreeing with God intellectually is simple, living out His Word is hard, in fact, impossible, apart from Holy Spirit.

Abraham's absolute obedience to the say-so of God enabled him to raise the knife to his son; he knew the heart of God and trusted in His Person, not just His promise. However, imagine the confusion, doubt, and fear that assayed Abraham on that dreaded walk to the altar of sacrifice. Now picture God whispering in his ear every heavy step, "Remember what I said...you will be the father of many nations through this very seed." Jesus, The Son of Man, was also trained to learn absolute trust in God. Hebrews 4:15 says He was tempted in every single way as we, except without sin. After a 40-day complete fast, famished and dehydrated, Satan tempted Jesus to prove His identity by turning a stone into bread. It was necessary for Jesus to eat the Word of God in that moment in order to be prepared to endure the Cross He would later bear. And though He was a Son, He learned obedience through suffering.

For Jesus, for Abraham, for us, God speaks in the middle of what we don't understand that we might know He is, I AM That I AM. Cling to God's Say-So as the final authority.

'you see our flaws, but I see you pure - you see your failures, I see the way you endure
you see your weakness but I see My Grace - covering you in glory beholding My face
when you see as I see then you'll be whole - My Lily of the Valley, you're the mate of My Soul'
Copyright 2007 RememberMEmore.com

Almighty God, I repent for elevating anything else above Your Word. I desire to unflinchingly believe Your say-so. Amen.

I am who He Says I am

picture

God's Word is so powerful He spoke forth creation.

ask

What is God saying about you that you need to agree with? Write it down and agree in faith.

pray

I am who He Says I am

Forgiveness By Heather Taylor

For if you forgive other people when they sin against you, your heavenly Father will also forgive you. But if you do not forgive others their sins, your Father will not forgive your sins. ~ Matthew 6: 14-15 (NIV)

Forgiveness was never easy for me. As a little girl, my mom said, "Tell your brother you forgive him!" looking at me with disdain when my weak attempt wasn't good enough. Glaring at me, her blue eyes squinting, she pursed her lips and demanded, "Now, act like you mean it!" I would look up at her, force a smile, and then do exactly as she said—act like I meant it.

As I became older, I continued to hold my enemies responsible for their transgressions. I didn't understand why God would want me to love my enemies. Someone, somewhere got it wrong. I continued to grow in my faith but eventually, I was faced with a clear decision—take the next step and trust God or lose my identity completely. Hate, like a weed, takes root and often goes unnoticed - until it's too late. Eventually, the weed is so large it consumes every thought and you are filled with anger, bitterness, and resentment. I ultimately could no longer control it. I started treating the people I loved the same way I treated my enemies. I hurt people in my life, including my husband and even myself.

When I finally realized why I was so miserable, I asked God to forgive me. It only took a second, forgiveness came and He showed me how to forgive others. I knew who I hated. I also knew why. Impossible to do on my own, I did the only thing I could do. Grabbing the oak table in the kitchen to steady myself, I cried out, "Lord, You say we must forgive to be forgiven, but I don't want to forgive! I'm angry and hurt. I don't want to forgive, but I do want to obey You. I can't do it Lord, but You can. Give me a heart to forgive." Once the words left my lips I could feel the hate leave my body. I was overcome with emotion and fell to the floor sobbing. I wasn't angry anymore, it felt amazing! My faith in God became stronger that day, and my desire to love people was ignited. God doesn't tell us to forgive others to hurt us, He wants us to forgive to save us from hurting ourselves.

Father, I ask You to help me forgive. Lord, search my heart and show me if there is anger or bitterness left unresolved. Give me the desire to love my enemies, Lord. Help me to do Your will instead of my own. Amen.

I am Forgiving

picture

Who in your life tends to trigger your anger? What would change if you forgave them?

ask

Are you willing to obey God and be set free by forgiving that person/people today?

pray

I am forgiving

A Step In Faith By Heather Taylor

When you fast, don't look like those who pretend to be spiritual. They want everyone to know they are fasting, so they appear in public looking miserable, gloomy, and disheveled. Believe me, they have already received their reward in full. When you fast, don't let it be obvious, but instead, wash your face and groom yourself and realize that your Father in the secret place is the one who is watching all that you do in secret and will continue to reward you openly." ~ Matthew 6:16-19 (NIV)

Fasting made no sense to me. Why would giving up food, something I love very much, make God happy? Maybe that question was never answered correctly for me in the past. Maybe, I was not willing to listen in the past. Either way, this year I took a step in faith and in doing so, my relationship with God grew.

Last January was the first time we started the New Year with our new church family, so we were not familiar with their custom of fasting for the first 21 days of the year. To my surprise, when our pastor spoke about it, I didn't become uncomfortable or upset, I became curious. He never insisted that the church as a whole must fast, but simply invited anyone to join them in some way. I prayed about it and was surprised to find that God, indeed, wanted me to participate. He even made it clear to me which things He wanted me to fast from for the 21 days.

Fasting, to me, always meant suffering. I couldn't understand why God would want us to do that. What I didn't know was that we don't suffer when we fast, we clear the way for God to communicate with us. All the distractions are gone and we can hear Him more clearly. I treasure the time I spent with God and the lessons I learned during my first 21-day fast. Nobody could have explained to me what fasting would do for my relationship with God and the clarity it gave me in realizing my identity and living my destiny.By saying yes to God and taking that leap of faith into fasting, I took one step closer to God, one step closer to my identity in Christ and received blessings and rewards from my Father, as He watched me from the secret place in Heaven.

Father, I ask You to speak to my heart and help me to discern what the next step in my journey with You may be. I ask You to always give me the desire to learn more about You and search Your Word for truth and the answers to my questions. Amen.

I am Rewarded

picture

Picture yourself successfully fasting and feeling closer to God. What does that look like?

ask

Would you consider a fast of your own? If so, ask God what He would like you to fast from and for how long.

pray

The Lord is My Provider By Nilda Campuzano

Therefore do not worry, saying 'What shall we eat?' or 'What shall we drink?' or 'What shall we wear?'
For your heavenly Father knows that you need all these things. ~ Matthew 6:31, 32b (NIV)

Growing up in Mexico gave me the opportunity to witness many small miracles, although I didn't know it at the time. Our life was very humble. Though I don't recall ever going hungry or lacking anything, I knew we had only the bare necessities. One day, my siblings and I were recalling our memories of the time an uncle gave us a huge bag of onions. Mom prepared the most delicious onion tacos anyone could enjoy! Soft corn tortillas filled with sauteed onions and salt, with a bit of salsa on top. We ate so many tacos, Mom was having a hard time keeping up. We went on and on, recounting that night, and asked Mom to make onion tacos again. Mom had been quiet. We realized she was holding back tears; she couldn't believe we remembered that night or that we loved those tacos so much. She revealed that she had absolutely nothing to feed us that night. She spent the day worrying about what to do because all she had was tortillas ... until my uncle showed up. Now she had tortillas and onions, so she did what Moms do—she cooked up a miracle.

At the time of this writing, my life is about to be uprooted completely. In a matter of weeks, I will move my children to a different house to create a home for them and to rebuild our family life from the ground up. My resources are limited, but my faith is not. Recalling one of the many miracles I witnessed as a child fills me with the joy of knowing that my Heavenly Father will provide all my needs!

Jesus plainly said that our Father knows what we need. He did not give us a list of things to do to make sure we were provided for; the only thing He asked was for us to look at the birds and the flowers and be assured. The same way I fully trusted my parents to provide for my needs as a child, Jesus calls me to trust in my Heavenly Father. As His daughter, I don't even have to ask; He knows what I need. All I have to do is trust.

Father, remind me that the same way You take care of the birds of the air and the lilies of the field, You will take care of all my needs; all I have to do is trust and rely on You. You are my provider. Amen.

I am Provided For

picture

Recall a time you experienced a blessing at the most unexpected time; nothing short of a miracle. Were you expecting God to come through? Or were you too busy trying to make it happen all on your own?

ask

Have I allowed God to show Himself to me as my Provider, or have I become so self-reliant that I miss the opportunity to be pampered by God?

pray

I am Provided For

The Gift Of Time By Lisa Danegelis

If you then, being evil, know how to give good gifts to your children, how much more will your Father who is in heaven give good gifts to those who ask Him! ~ Matthew 7:11 (NKJV)

"I love you more than ... " I'm sure you have played this game with your kids! Secret gestures and words were daily rituals as my kids were growing up. As the game escalated, my son would not be outwitted or out-loved! We had already raced through favorite foods and all sorts of adjectives when we arrived at the planets ... we sailed through those on our race to out-love one another. His face lit up as he said, "I love you farther than ... than ... than ... Zeba!" This imaginary planet became our secret code as we drew a quick "Z" through the air, a gesture that still resonates for us both years later.

God and I have our special secrets as well. The first time He called me "Honey" I gasped and said, "That's what my Dad used to call me!" He said, "I know," and I absorbed His love while sensing Him smiling over me. As I bustle about my day He often whispers, "My girl," and I respond, "My God." There is such a deep intimacy it nearly takes my breath away. Late at night, when sleep is elusive, I picture my "Daddy" sitting in the comfy chair in the corner of my bedroom. I tell Him everything as I ramble on, tripping over my racing thoughts. We giggle, reminisce and grieve together; sometimes we just sit in silence. He is so patient, kind and forgiving... it is so easy being with Him; "Easy As a Sunday Morning," using the singer, Lionel Richie's lyrics.

Rereading my own words makes me realize how often I unknowingly put our personal God on the sidelines of my life thinking He is too busy, not interested or maybe too displeased with me to care. Oh, my! Now the tears are flowing! My precious Lord, I am so sorry for not including You in every moment! Nothing I do or say chases you away! Nothing! You deserve my full devotion, attention and abandoned love! I want to open my eyes in the morning and know You are there waiting to wink at me and share every moment of my day. One of the most beautiful "gifts" the Father gives us is His time and unconditional acceptance. We are His joy and delight. He adores celebrating life with us! May we revel in the time spent together as much as He does.

Father, what a joy to know You delight in spending time with me! Help me to include You in every area of my life. Amen.

I am Out-Loved

picture

How can you begin to cultivate gratefulness in every moment of your life by remembering that God has already given you good gifts?

ask

Matthew 7:11 says that our Father will give us good gifts if we ask Him. What are you asking from Him today?

pray

I am Out-Loved

A House Divided By Nilda Campuzano

Jesus knew their thoughts and said to them, 'Every kingdom divided against itself is brought to desolation, and every city or house divided against itself will not stand.' ~ Matthew 12:25 (NKJV)

If we were to spend some time together, you would find that my love languages are words of encouragement, closely followed by acts of service. Service was learned by watching my mother and grandmother come alive when preparing delicious Mexican dishes for visitors. My mother is at her best when she finds practical ways to help others, and everyone who ever visited my mom left feeling energized and nurtured. Speaking words of encouragement was learned by default. I was often the victim of vicious verbal attacks that left deep marks on how I viewed myself. Experiencing the devastating effects of ill words gave me a keen awareness of the power of what I say, so I strive to remind people of all the goodness that is in them.

Recently, I was confronted with the reality that even though I extend words of encouragement and acts of service to many people around me, I do not extend myself the same courtesy. Quite often I make the mistake of overcommitting to the point that I neglect to take good care of myself. Balancing family and work can be daunting, and in an effort to take care of everything, I run myself ragged. Likewise, with words of encouragement, it is quite easy for me to see goodness in other people, but I struggle to recognize it in myself. I tend to be overly critical of my actions and show myself very little mercy when I make mistakes.

Jesus stated in Matthew 12:25 that a household divided against itself will not stand, and I have experienced this first-hand. When we are unaware of the negative ways we think about ourselves or the demeaning words we speak to ourselves, we are divided against ourselves. And a house divided will fall. It is not the will of God for us to serve and encourage others while neglecting our own mental, physical, and emotional well being. If our cups are to overflow, we must first allow them to be filled with love, acceptance, forgiveness, grace, and mercy. Allow God to show you the ways in which your inner house is divided, and allow His grace to fill you up to overflowing. Ask God to transform you into a house built firmly on His rock, a steadfast and welcoming place for all - including yourself.

Dear Jesus, help me to love myself the way I love others. Please grant me the grace to see me, as You see me, and to love myself and others from a pure heart.

I am Built on the Rock

picture

What would the reaction of your friends and loved ones be if you spoke to them the way you speak to yourself and treat them the way you treat yourself?

ask

If I asked you to make a list of everyone you love, what number would you occupy on that list?

pray

Growth By Heather Taylor

A farmer went out to sow his seed. As he was scattering the seed, some fell along the path; it was trampled on, and the birds ate it up. Some fell on rocky ground, and when it came up, the plants withered because they had no moisture. Other seeds fell among the thorns, which grew up with it and choked the plants. Still, other seeds fell on good soil. It came up and yielded a crop, a hundred times more than was sown." When he said this, he called out "Whoever has ears to hear, let them hear.
~ Matthew 13:1-9 (NIV)

Every New Year I pray for God to give me a word that represents what I should work on for that year. In the past, the Lord has always found a unique way to reveal this word, sharing one word that shows up often and clearly. This year, after I prayed for my word, I waited expectantly looking for it to show up somewhere surprising. It never did. After about a week, I got a little less patient and asked God to reveal my word again. I waited, even less patiently, but nothing happened. Finally, New Year's Eve had arrived and I still didn't have my word. I was pretty disappointed. I knew it was just a word, but to me, it represented more than that.

That evening, my husband and I were at church when our pastor asked the congregation to think about how we would make a difference in the new year. I thought about my word and silently asked God again, to please reveal it to me. When the service was almost over, we all stood and got ready to receive communion. Our pastor said, "Ask for a supernatural experience as you take communion." I remember my words exactly, "Lord, please clearly tell me what you want from me this year. Help me to know what direction you want me to go and what you want me to do."

When the bread touched my lips, my mind began to play like a movie clip from the past two weeks. Flashes ran across my mind of a recitation of the parable of the farmer and the seeds, then to a book I was reading about a farmer planting seeds in different soils, and finally, to my pastor teaching on the importance of planting seeds in good soil (Luke 8:5-8). At once, I knew my word! It was GROWTH. God not only gave me my word, but he included verses to explain exactly how that growth would be possible—by having a heart that was good soil. I was so overjoyed, I was laughing right there during communion! The word growth symbolizes my journey and how far I've already come, but it also shows me the future and how much more God has planned for me. Because of who I am in Christ, I look forward to so much growth!

Father God, I pray that You would continue to grow me in every area of my life. I want to always be good soil and to produce good fruit. I pray Lord that I can be an example of a good and faithful servant. Amen.

I am Good Soil

picture

Picture your heart as good soil, and the seeds planted are the Word of God. What is growing in your garden?

ask

In what ways have you grown most in your identity in Christ?

pray

I am Good Soil

Who Do You Say I Am? By Nilda Campuzano

When Jesus came to the region of Caesarea he asked his disciples, "Who do people say the Son of Man is?" They replied, "Some say John the Baptist; others say Elijah; still others, Jeremiah or one of the prophets." "But what about you?" he asked, "Who do you say I am?" ~ Matthew 16:13-15

Have you ever been asked the question, "Who are you?" This is one of the hardest questions to answer. We try to define ourselves by what we do, who we are related to, or our accomplishments. In today's social media-driven world, we might even be tempted to define ourselves by the number of followers we have.

Every time I heard a sermon based on Matthew 16:13-15, I wondered why Jesus asked this question. It seems out of place that Jesus would ask this, as he unequivocally stated so many times that He was the Son of God, the Savior. Why was He all of a sudden interested in knowing what people were saying about Him? Was He in need of reassurance of his ministry? Was He undergoing a sudden identity crisis?

None of the above. I believe the reason He asked that question is that in its answer, we actually find our identity. When Jesus asked Peter, "Who do you say I am?" Peter answered: "You are the Son of God." For me, answering Jesus' question demanded that I confront what others told me about Him, the concepts I developed as I went through life, and the lies that the enemy spoon-fed me every time my life went south. I pray that you, as Peter did, recognize Jesus as the Son of God, as the greatest gift God gave the world, and as the Savior that will guide you to everlasting life. Then you will hear Jesus say as He said to Peter, "Blessed are you, for this was not revealed to you by flesh and blood, but by my Father in Heaven."

Dear Jesus, for more than 2,000 years, people have been hearing about You, but very few have actually come to know You. I want to stop hearing about You, and experience You first hand. Grant that I would see You for who You really are. Reveal to me the truth of who You are. Amen.

I am Found in Him

picture

Put aside everything anyone has told you about Jesus. From very personal experience answer this: Who do you say He is?

ask

How has your opinion or concept of Jesus been tainted by what others have said or done?

pray

I am Found in Him

My Great Adventure By Heather Taylor

For even the Son of Man did not come to be served, but to serve, and to give his life as a ransom to many. ~ Mark 10:45 (NIV)

Learning who I am in Christ, my true identity, has been an adventure. God has taken me on a journey where I learn a new and wonderful thing about who I really am at each destination. My favorite stop was the one that surprised me the most.

During my time as a "part-time follower," I would attempt to go to church on and off throughout the year. I hate to admit it, but I never really enjoyed attending church. I often found myself daydreaming during the messages and comparing the purple shoes to my left to the pair of orange shoes to my right. I would wonder if the curly hair in front of me was natural or a perm? I did everything you could do to entertain myself while sitting in a pew—except listen to the message. When the music cued to close the service, I was always the first to leave and ran straight through the groups that would gather and linger. I would have one hand pulling my child behind me and the other stretched out in front of me ready to open doors. I didn't want to talk to anyone or listen to someone asking me to sign up for something. It wasn't that I hated everyone, I just liked being left alone.

After several years, God led me to a local church down the road from my home. We had been attending the new church for two short months when I started to have the strangest feelings. I found myself enjoying the people around me. Every time I would visit a new ministry area of the church, I felt the desire to serve there. Instead of rushing out the door when the service was over and the music would play, I felt sad that it was over! I remember saying to my husband one night, "What in the world is wrong with me?" I was clearly undergoing a significant transformation. God was calling me into service and revealing another part of my identity in Him: I am a servant, just like Jesus! And so are you! You were made to serve, just as Christ came to serve us.

Lord, I pray that you will show me how and where I can serve. Activate the gifts You've placed in me for the service of others. Allow me to be a vessel to show your love through service. Amen.

I am a Servant

picture

Picture yourself serving the Body of Christ. Where do you feel drawn to help? Why?

ask

What are your gifts and have they been activated to serve others? What is one step you can take in that direction?

pray

I am a Servant

Blessed is She By Joni Jones

Blessed is she who has believed that the Lord would fulfill His promises to her! ~ Luke 1:45

I am Blessed, not because of what I have or what good has come into my life but because God calls me blessed. I used to believe that when I got what I wanted when I wanted it, then I was blessed. Blessed when I received an unexpected gift, or when my husband said, "I do," or when my children were born, or when I fit into those jeans. Oh yes, these are all blessings but I didn't receive them because I deserved them.

Blessed is so much more. Being blessed is not believing in the actual blessing, but rather in the One who wants to pour out His gifts wrapped up in His promises on His Daughter. Blessings that can't be touched, but can touch our hearts with His transforming power. In the "Bible Sense Lexicon, blessed means "characterized by happiness and being highly favored, as by divine grace."

Blessed is she who believes that she is highly favored, who is fearlessly bold in being herself because she is His Daughter. Blessed is she who lives as chosen, adopted, accepted, redeemed and forgiven, because of a God who always keeps His promises. Blessed is she who believes she has an Abba Father who embraces her with an unconditional love that He has promised to her from the very beginning, "We love Him because He first loved us" (I John 4:19NIV). Blessed are we in Him who is love. Blessed are we who have permission to live as His masterpiece, no matter what we feel, or do, or what our circumstances are, or what blessings that we can physically see and touch. Blessed are you, who is a recipient of Christ's identity, as you continue believing.

Dear Lord, thank You for calling me blessed. Whether or not I feel like I am blessed, You have poured out Your favor and grace upon my life through the sacrifice of Jesus. I thank You for the blessings of unconditional love, forgiveness, mercy, and redemption. Amen.

I am Blessed

picture

What promise of God do you need to receive and believe?

ask

If believing who we are in Christ is being blessed, how are you able to press forward as one who is highly favored?

pray

Peacefully Becoming By Joni Jones

Daughter, your faith has healed you. Go in peace. ~ Luke 8:48 (NIV)

Striving to arrive at being the perfect Christian will always be a constant effort, particularly when I believe I can be so much better than who I think I am. I fail. Arriving is an impossibility because I never attain the perfection that I crave. I always fall short, even of who He says I am when I don't believe what He says about me. Striving to arrive is how I live at times, despite my believing that Jesus loves me, from the moment He healed my brokenness, setting me free from a life filled with self-loathing and condemnation.

I have been walking with Jesus for decades, yet something was blocking my heart to fully embrace and live out my identity in Him. It has become clearer now, it's when I strive to do what only He can do—striving to arrive to be just like Him. The closer I get to Jesus, the more I need of Him, as He is removing more of that part of me that tends to strive. Jesus calls me to constant surrender while living as His daughter. He is relentlessly changing me more into the likeness of Jesus, like a piece of clay on the Potter's wheel becoming who He has created me to be - His daughter. Being made into His daughter brings growing pains at times, as it is a process. He is molding me into the likeness of His Son, so I no longer strive, only allow the Potter to do His work. There is an undeniable growth when I choose to walk boldly in His peace as His daughter because I know that I am one of His favored ones.

Walking is a choice, whether forward, backward or standing still. To walk forward as His daughter, we must replace "striving to arrive" with "becoming," choosing to never be stagnant. Striving to arrive is part of the past now, as I am evolving, step by step, walking as His daughter. As His daughters, we have the honor to walk forward in our claimed identity as His, as He continues to shape us into who we are becoming. Believe in Him. Be bold in Him. Be blessed in Him, because Daughter, your faith has healed you. Go in peace. (Luke 8:48)

Jesus, thank you for equipping me by putting
Your strength within me. Amen.

I am on the Potter's Wheel

picture

What new truth do you need to claim as a Daughter as you walk forward
surrendered in Your Potter's Hands?

ask

How would you describe the process of being shaped into the likeness of
Jesus? What do you need to surrender to the Potter so that you can boldly
walk forward in your new identity?

pray

I am on the Potter's Wheel

Authority Over the Power of the Enemy By Susan Tyler

I have given you authority to trample on snakes and scorpions and to overcome all the power of the enemy; nothing will harm you. ~ Luke 10:19 (NIV)

It started as a typical work morning until I received an urgent call from the President of the company, who was also my direct supervisor. I immediately went down to his office, and my world began to crumble. He informed me that one of my employees, my assistant manager, had filed a harassment claim against me. "Who me? Are you sure?" was all I could ask. The accusation came totally out of left field and was not in alignment with my twenty-plus years of stellar corporate work experience. My boss began to ask me questions and notified me that he would have to complete a formal investigation, including interviewing several of my colleagues and all members of my staff! I was overwhelmed; a wide array of emotions, including shock, unbelief, confusion, fear, and anger began to overtake my body.

As I began to walk back to my office, the Holy Spirit spoke to me reminding me He would fight this battle. Suddenly, a warrior spirit replaced the onslaught of emotion. I was in the midst of a spiritual war; which could only be fought and won in the Heavenly realm. I began to pray to God for guidance and to proclaim, no weapon formed against me shall prosper, according to Isaiah 54:17. Every day, I positioned myself for the battle. I arrived early to work during the investigation. Steadfast, I entered my department praising God, thanking Him for reigning in my life and the organizational life of the company that I worked for. Without telling a soul, I anointed all doors and windows with oil while loudly proclaiming that God had given me the authority to stomp out my enemies. I fought back and reminded the devil that he had already lost the war! The victory was mine because Jesus said so. Three weeks later, I was completely vindicated!

As we go about our daily lives, we will undoubtedly face trials time and time again. However, we can walk in victory, knowing that God has already provided us with the authority to overpower the enemy—today and always.

Father, throughout the Bible, including in Exodus 14:14, 2 Chronicles 20:17, Deuteronomy 20:4, Deuteronomy 3:22, Deuteronomy 1:30, Isaiah 54:17, Psalm 34:17, Psalm 144:1, Ephesians 6:10, and Isaiah 43:2, you remind us that you will fight our battles. This enables us to have authority over the dominance of our enemies. During this trial, guide me in the way that I should proceed, and I thank You ahead of time for the victory. In Jesus' Name, I pray, Amen.

I am Authorized

picture

Can you think about a battle that you are currently facing or have dealt with in the past? Who is your real enemy? How will you fight him effectively?

ask

Look up the Scriptures in the prayer. In the future, how will these Scriptures help you to fight for the victory when you are faced with life's challenges?

pray

I am Authorized

Childlike Faith By Heidi Sampson

Do not be afraid, little flock, for your Father has chosen gladly to give you the kingdom.
~ Luke 12:32 (NASB)

In my time working with foster kids, there was one boy, Jacob, who God used to teach me an important lesson. Jacob lived with us for a while and he had special needs. Jacob had the body of a fifth-grader with the mind of a first-grader. Jacob did not know an earthly dad. He was separated from his family. The first few nights with us he cried to go home. He did not understand why he had to "move away to foster care." Yet Jacob brought us so much joy.

Around the time when Jacob lived with us, Chris Tomlin's song, Good Good Father, came out. Jacob liked music, but he LOVED that song. Requesting we play the song, he would jump up and down singing, and he would sing it to himself in the shower. This precious child of God met his Heavenly Father through these words. Jacob's eyes lit up each time he would sing, "You're a good, good Father .. and I'm loved by You, it's who I am. . . You are perfect in all of Your ways. . ." Jacob would raise his hands, stomp his foot and sway his body to this song as it was repeated in our home. Never quite on key, Jacob sang loudly without a care in the world. His involuntary response to his Father was such a beautiful picture of complete surrender. By the world's standard, this kid has nothing to offer: he is behind in school, his family depends on government money, his mental capacity is not what it 'should' be.

But Jacob is wiser and richer than any person on earth because he knows and lives in his identity as a child of God. Our Father has gladly chosen to give His kingdom to Jacob because of his faith in God. That boy will forever hold a special place in my heart for teaching me what it means to accept who I am and who made me. Our Jacob came to accept Christ into his heart before he moved back home. I have not been able to see him since he left our care, but I am overjoyed to know that I will get to meet up again with him in Heaven. Join me as I stand with him, stomp my foot, and raise my hand to sing to our good, good Father!

Thank You for being my Father, for knowing me, for loving me,
and for giving me Your Kingdom. Allow me to accept all that
You have for me today. Amen.

I am given the Kingdom

picture

Jot down positive qualities about yourself. At the bottom of the list write
"Being loved by God is who I am."

ask

What aspects of your life do you feel you do not measure up? Are there
things you have not given over to God because you may feel inadequate?

pray

I am given the Kingdom

Listening to God By Susan Tyler

The apostles said to the Lord, 'Increase our faith!' He replied, 'If you have faith as small as a mustard seed, you can say to this mulberry tree, Be uprooted and planted in the sea, and it will obey you.
~ Luke 17:5-6 (NIV)

Several years ago, I had to step out on faith after hearing God's voice. I was unhappy at work. The toxicity in the environment was overwhelming; I would cry on Sunday evenings knowing I had to go to work the next morning. For months my doctor tried to get me to take time off work because I was clinically depressed. I refused to listen to her advice; as the Director of Human Resources, I knew that taking time off from work was not a good career move. Besides, I was a single parent and needed the job to pay my bills. Around the same time, God began to speak to me, saying, "Leave your job." For three long months, I ignored His quiet, yet firm voice. I refused to believe that He would instruct me to do something that sounded so ridiculous; like quitting my job! The work environment continued to weigh heavily on me, and four months after I first heard God's voice, I finally did it; I quit my job. All my friends wondered about my sanity because I walked away without a plan or any other source of income. Up until that point, I had a stellar career and had never done anything that would appear to be so irresponsible in my life! From an outsider's perspective, my world was crumbling at a fast pace, yet internally, I had perfect peace because I was certain that I was obeying God's instructions.

Exactly two weeks later, I became self-employed when a colleague recommended me for a year-long consulting assignment which ended up lasting three years! Supernaturally, God turned my mourning into dancing and all He required of me was to step out in faith. Often when we are faced with a difficult task or challenge, we become paralyzed with fear because we only see the challenge through our limited ability to rise above the situation. Our reliance is on ourselves; not on God.

That is what Jesus spoke to the disciples about. Because He (Jesus) had a relationship with them, He expected them to have faith that He would help them perform the tasks He had given them, and you know what? He expects the same amount of faith from you and me.

My Father, thank You for allowing me to share Your Heart with your daughter today. I know You put these words in front of her today and I pray You will open her heart and ears to hear what You have been saying to her. I pray that she will hear Your call and will obey Your instructions.

I am Full of Faith

picture

Picture Jesus as the Good Shepherd from Psalm 23. Imagine Him guiding you through that difficult place just as a shepherd guides his sheep. See yourself following His lead in faith and obedience. Describe what situation in your life He is guiding you through.

ask

What is something God has placed in your heart to do but you've been hesitating in your obedience? What are the reasons you are hesitating? Will you trust God with those reasons today?

pray

Loved on Purpose By Joni Jones

For God so loved the world that He gave His one and only Son, that whoever believes in Him shall not perish but have eternal life. ~ John 3:16

"Do you love me?" This has been the cry of my heart. I wouldn't utter the words, but it was through my actions that I was seeking the answer. As a doer, if I do enough then I will be loved enough, which backfired every time. Then I heard the words, "I have loved you," says the Lord. "But you ask, 'How have You loved us?' (Malachi 1:2) Israel doubted God's Love, too.

"I have loved you," says the Lord. But you ask, " Why didn't You give me this, or change that?"

"I have loved you," says the Lord. But you ask, "Where were You when this happened and when I was left alone?

"I have loved you," says the Lord. But you ask, "Why didn't you answer my prayers in my way?"

"I have loved you," says the Lord, "from the very moment once upon a time ago when I knit you together in your mother's womb for a purpose." (Psalm 139:13)

"For God so loved" that once upon a time, He purposely created each one of us. His choice. And now He gives us a choice, "Whoever believes in Him shall not perish but have eternal life" (John 3:16) to live happily ever after in eternal bliss. To be born again. Our decision. Our forever life. Covered in Jesus, all because God said, "I have loved you." Born on purpose. Live on purpose. Loved on purpose. Love isn't based on whether you believe it or not, but because He said, "I have loved you." And we reply, Thank You!

Thank You, God, for knitting me together on that one day You chose just for me. Thank You for allowing me to continue to live forever as yours, as I ask Jesus to come into my heart so that He can love me perfectly as You created me to be.

I am Loved Sacrificially

picture

How does your believing in God's ultimate gift of love that lasts beyond this life, change the way you will live your day?

ask

If God tells you that He loves you, what gets in the way of your receiving His love?

pray

I am Loved Sacrificially

Pressing Forward By Joni Jones

Then Jesus said to him, "Get up! Pick up your mat and walk". At once the man was cured; he picked up his mat and walked. ~ John 5:8-9

What do you do when you know the truth that you are loved by God and that your identity is in Him—when you know it in your head, but you don't know how to live it? Now is time to walk as His daughter. When Jesus healed the sick woman (Luke 8:48), He immediately called her by her new name, daughter. Jesus then said, "GO in peace." Later in Jesus' ministry, He also told the lame man something similar, "pick up your mat and walk."

One day God shed His truth on my wounded soul when I heard those same words, "Pick up your mat and walk." I followed the directive and picked up my mat and starting walking, however, I realized I kept all the stuff from my past in an old backpack that I continued to carry on my shoulders. And then the lightbulb went on! Why would I still carry what was weighing me down? I then pictured myself literally shaking my past off, it was not me anymore. But who was I now that I couldn't carry my past? I wondered how does one walk as a new creation? The only way was to walk wobbly, as I felt like a toddler taking her first steps, organically pressing forward into unchartered territory.

That is how we do it, every moment, as God is continually transforming us into the likeness of His Son. Jesus says, "Go in peace." I think He means FLY as if you really believe you are a beautiful butterfly even though you feel like a caterpillar. So many of us find ourselves like the lame man, wanting to find healing or peace, yet we tend to look everywhere but to the one source that can heal. Jesus asked the question, "Do you want to get well?" The man did, yet he needed Jesus. Permission to walk was granted. We, too, have permission to live and walk as a new creation, in all He says we are! We have permission to leave behind our mat and our backpacks full of past hurts and regrets. Get up and walk! Better yet, run boldly as His daughter, restored, renewed and redeemed, just because Jesus says so.

Lord, help me to run boldly as Your daughter, willing to drop everything from the past that hinders me from going where You call me. Amen.

I am Free of the Past

picture

How would you walk differently through your day believing that you are a new creation who Jesus has restored, renewed and redeemed?

ask

What burdens from the past do you carry on your back that are keeping you from walking as a daughter?

pray

I Have Rivers of Living Water! By Sue Sherstad

All you thirsty ones, come to Me! Come to Me and drink! Believe in Me so that rivers of living water will burst out from within you, flowing from your innermost being, just like the Scripture says!
~ John 7:38 (TPT)

I remember the special night I was filled with this living water. I had been saved for five months and water baptized when a dear friend, Pearl, invited me to her church. Little did I know that my life would be changed, and I was about to receive the most beautiful spiritual gift outside of salvation! This river of living water transformed me from the inside out. The Holy Spirit is this river. He is the spirit and life of God. He empowered me to overcome great adversity in my life, teaching me and bringing revelation to my heart as I spent time in the word of God. Chains of fear were broken, and I became free to pursue the dreams the Lord had put in my heart.

He is a friend and comforter that carried me through dark and lonely nights, through my season of singleness, waiting for my future husband to arrive. He was there the night I was alone with my two-year-old daughter who was sick with a high fever. As I prayed, He gave me a song to sing of the spirit and the fever broke! I experience His presence washing over me like a river during times of intimate worship. There's nothing in this world that can compare to being filled with the Spirit.

Jesus' invitation is to all believers to come and receive the living water that satisfies our thirsty souls. This water is poured out on us by the Holy Spirit to bring refreshing to tired and stressed-out minds and bodies. It will drive away depression and release a wellspring of joy and peace that anchors us in the storms of life. The Holy Spirit has been poured out not just for our benefit, but also to be released and overflow into the lives of those around us. As my husband and I have pastored and ministered, we have seen the sick made whole, the captive set free, and the broken-hearted restored. Jesus wants to give you this river of living water. Are you thirsty for more? All you have to do is ask and He will fill you to overflowing!

Lord, I thirst for more of You. Give me this river of living water that I might experience the fullness of Your joy and strength in my life. Fill me to overflowing and use me for your glory! Amen.

I am Filled with His Spirit

picture

What would it look like for you to be filled with His Spirit today? How will asking for more of His living water change your life?

ask

In what ways have you experienced this living water? Are you thirsty for more? Tell God what you need more of.

pray

A New Definition of Success By Eleanor Weldie

Jesus spoke to the Pharisees again. He said, 'I am the light of the world. Whoever follows me will have a life filled with light and will never live in the dark.' ~ John 8:12 (GW)

What is your definition of success? It can look different in everyone's life, and no one is immune to the suffocating feeling of not reaching their personal goals. When I was in college, I went through a brief period where I thought I could make myself into a runner. I would lace up my tennis shoes every morning at 6 AM, throw on a peppy playlist, and jog around campus as the sun came up in a splendor of pink and blues. This lasted for... about two weeks. The weather got colder, my classes started piling on more homework, and, to be perfectly honest, I just liked the idea of sleeping in. I didn't reach my goal of making myself a runner. I never wore out my Nikes, beat a personal record, or ran a half-marathon. I was wholly unsuccessful as a runner.

I think we can often get down on ourselves about the things we are "unsuccessful" at. If our hair isn't perfectly curled, if the kids aren't sitting down nicely for a meal, if the house has too much dog-hair piled up in corners, or if the lovely girl in the pew next to us sings better than we do at church, we become easily discouraged. Can I tell you a secret?

God doesn't see us as unsuccessful.

He measures success differently. He calls us to live lives filled with light because He measures success in light. We are light when we look for Him and His wisdom wholeheartedly. When we are faithful, as He has called us to be. We are light when we display kindness to our neighbor. When we persevere and strive to strengthen His Kingdom. When we show up to church even when we don't want to. When we tell others about our Father through our actions and our words. Jesus is the light of the world. If we have Him, we live lives filled with light; we need not fear failure. Instead, we can hold to the promise that we are salt and light because that's what Jesus calls us in Matthew 5:13-16. We get to reflect the light that He is, and that, my friends, is success.

Father, thank You for Your great light in the world. Thank You that Jesus calls me to live in the light and not the darkness and that You only ask me to live for You. Remind me that a life lived fully in You is success.

I am a Success

picture

How can your definition of success be modified to fit with Jesus' definition of living in the light?

ask

Why is it important to live as salt and light in this world?

pray

I am a Success

Stopping to Rest By Heidi Sampson

He came to Simon Peter, who said to him, 'Lord, are you going to wash my feet?' Jesus replied 'You do not realize now what I am doing, but later you will understand.' ~ John 13:6-7 (NIV)

My boys came running into the house one afternoon to tell me they found a hummingbird trapped in our garage. Being a science teacher, I know hummingbirds cannot see long distances. Due to their size and quick movements, hummingbirds struggle to see a larger perspective. It is not flying into a garage that causes their demise, but their inability to slow down and see where they are. They repeatedly run into the garage walls until they are tired and overheated. Their small bodies can't handle this intense work, and they eventually wear out. If those birds were to pause momentarily, they could turn to fly back into the environment they thrive in. So with my kids watching wide-eyed, I grabbed the bird and held it, forcing it to pause. After a brief rest, the hummingbird flew in the right direction.

My life parallels this predicament. I am often 'flapping my wings' relentlessly to prove I am capable. Despite exhaustion, I continue slamming into the wall because I am trapped. My busyness is unfulfilling and anxiety-ridden. In the book, Life of the Beloved, Henri Nouwen says we live "in a world filled with voices that shout: You are no good, you are ugly; you are worthless; you are despicable, you are nobody—unless you can demonstrate the opposite." So with me, I am attempting to demonstrate my worth; some days it nearly kills me. I am that hummingbird hitting my garage wall again and again in order to establish who I am.

Then God puts His gentle, but firm hands on me. In the midst of my striving, He forces me to pause to rest in His strength. His tender voice tells me I am enough. When He comes to calm me, I feel like Peter who did not grasp what Jesus was doing by washing his feet. Not until after Jesus' resurrection did Peter comprehend what Jesus did. It is difficult to understand why God wants me to be still, but I am learning to listen to God's quiet voice. He knows the next step in my journey. and I do not need to prove my worth. Jesus' disciples had to grieve the loss of their friend before they saw the result of His crucifixion. Even when circumstances seem impossible, God has a plan. We do not have to know the whole story in order to trust His sovereignty.

Lord, may I feel Your hands around me today. Allow me to get past my striving and panic to feel Your true rest. Thank you for forcing me to stop and breathe in order to find myself in You. Amen.

I am Free to Rest

picture

Sit in God's presence and listen for His quiet voice.

ask

How is God forcing you to rest? What are you trying to prove about yourself?

pray

I am Free to Rest

Meet My Best Friend By Heather Taylor

All this I have spoken while still with you. But the Advocate, the Holy Spirit, whom the Father will send in my name, will teach you all things and will remind you of everything I have said. ~ John 14:25-26 (NIV)

On my journey to claiming my identity in Christ, I had to face the painful reality that some of the people I had chosen to do life with weren't meant to be a part of my life. I slowly started trimming my friendship tree. Some limbs were already dead; the wood already rotten and hollow. These limbs hadn't produced fruit in years, so they weren't hard to remove. Other branchlets still had green leaves and they fought to stay connected to the tree. The problem was they had been producing bad fruit. In order to save the tree, they had to go. By the time all the pruning was done, I felt like an oak tree in the middle of winter whose leaves had fallen and been blown away with only bark and broken limbs left and exposed to the bitter cold. I felt completely alone and left to wonder if I had done the right thing.

Eventually, God delivered a new tribe of women in my life that were real friends. The differences between the relationships I had then and the ones I have now is night and day. But, I was also different. I learned a secret. When Jesus walked on the earth He told us He was leaving but in His place, He was leaving something "even better" than Himself (John 16:7). He left so that we can receive the Holy Spirit! If I'm honest, I really had no idea what that meant, but once I decided to dive in and find out, I quickly realized that Jesus left us a best friend! The Holy Spirit isn't a 'THE', He is just Holy Spirit like I am Heather. He lives inside us; if we invite Him in. He loves us, guides us, talks to us (no, I'm not crazy), and wants nothing more than to be our best friend.

Jesus left us so that HS (that's my nickname for Him) can stay and be with us forever. He gives us power, love, protection, discipline, guidance and He is a great listener! Friends are great and I love mine—but HS is our connection to God. He continues to teach us our identity in Christ. You never have to be alone again because Jesus made sure when He ascended to Heaven He sent an advocate to stay with us forever. Get to know your real best friend. Get to know HS!

Holy Spirit, I thank you for living inside of us. I pray that you will continue to guide me. Lord, remind me throughout the day that the Holy Spirit is with me and that nothing is too small or too big to seek His guidance. Amen.

I am Holy Spirit's Friend

picture

Picture yourself in an intimate friendship with the Holy Spirit. What would that look like?

ask

How would staying connected with Holy Spirit make your daily life different?

pray

I am Holy Spirit's Friend

Stay By Traci Weldie

Remain in me, as I also remain in you. No branch can bear fruit by itself; it must remain in the vine. Neither can you bear fruit unless you remain in me. "I am the vine; you are the branches. If you remain in me and I in you, you will bear much fruit; apart from me you can do nothing." ~ John 15:4 (NIV)

I have a hard time staying put; I'm a mover. Not in the ADHD sense; more in the way that I am constantly thinking up the next thing I want to do or place I want to go. I have moved often and sense myself longing for new spaces, new outlooks, and new landscapes. Sadly, this characteristic of longing to be on the move has seeped into my spiritual life. Even when I know where I find peace and contentment, joy and blessing, my flesh causes me to wonder, "Is this all there is? Is there anything better?" I think of the beautiful hymn, "Come Thou Fount of Every Blessing" where the hymnist pens, "Prone to wander, Lord I feel it. Prone to leave the God I love." I relate! Every time I sing those piercing words, my heart crumbles and I cry out to God, "Why do I do this?"

Jesus encouraged his disciples to remain because He remains in us. How amazing it is to know that the God of the universe has promised to stay no matter how we are feeling, what mistakes we have made, or what doubts are running through our minds! God stays. He does not leave. He simply asks us to do the same. Stay. Don't leave. He is the vine, we are the branches. A beautiful aspect of being a branch is that we cannot remove ourselves from the vine; despite all we might do to leave, the vine will hold tight to its branches.

Jesus says that staying with Him the way He stays with us is the only way we can bear fruit. He even further saying, " ... apart from me, you can do NOTHING." I have asked God to use me; send me; cause me to bear fruit. I realize unless I STAY with Him, I will bear no evidence of being His branch. Sadly, I have tasted and seen that apart from Him, not only can I accomplish nothing—I've got nothing! What an amazing blessing to know that He never leaves us! So, I delight in knowing that the only work I need to do is STAY. So today, I will STAY in communication with God, I will STAY focused on seeing His beautiful creation around me, I will STAY with the God I love.

Dear Lord, I long to stay with You. I am so blessed that You promised to abide with me if I stay with You. Help me to remain. Amen.

I am His Branch

picture

How has your life looked differently when you have actively abided with Jesus than times when you have not?

ask

What are three practical steps you can take to ensure abiding in Jesus this week?

pray

From Head to Heart and Out into the World By Amy Oaks

"I am the vine; you are the branches. If you remain in Me and I in you, you will bear much fruit; apart from Me you can do nothing. If you do not remain in Me, you are like a branch that is thrown away and withers; such branches are picked up, thrown into the fire, and burned. If you remain in Me and my words remain in you, ask whatever you wish, and it will be done for you. This is to my Father's glory, that you bear much fruit, showing yourselves to be my disciples." ~ John 15:5-8 (NIV)

I was raised in a traditional Lutheran church where I learned rote memorization and all the usual Bible stories. I was baptized, confirmed, and married there, my dad was confirmed and married there, and his parents were founding members. My parents raised me in this church, doing all the right things to bring me up with strong roots in faith. Why then, could I attend an entire church service while my mind wandered, and not remember much about it? Why then, when I left home, did I leave religion behind, relieved that my Sunday mornings were free?

I realize now that I had plenty of head knowledge about God and the Bible, but I had yet to invite the Holy Spirit into my heart, much less integrate Him into my life. Like a branch barely attached to the vine, I was spiritually malnourished, withering, and empty inside. No way could I bear fruit or begin to fulfill His purposes for me!

Eventually, a series of events led us to feel very lost and far from God at our church. We made the difficult decision to leave and find a new place for our family to worship and grow. We were eventually led to a different church where we found a new enthusiasm for the Lord, and wonderful mentors to guide us forward in faith. I finally understood what it felt like to praise God; not just go through the motions. I learned to pray, then listen for the Holy Spirit to answer. I learned to surrender to Him instead of believing that I alone controlled all of life's circumstances. Slowly, all that head knowledge began to trickle down into my heart. My lifeline to Christ's vine became stronger, and I could at last be who He meant me to be all along, out in the world.

Dear God, It's not enough to know about You, we need to be connected to You as one with our hearts through living in Your Word and surrendering to Your love for us. Help us surrender to You, and find our true selves in Your calling. Amen

I am Connected to God

picture

Where are your connections to Him weakened, and how can you grow them?

ask

Why do we need to be connected to Christ's lifeline?

pray

I am Connected to God

Joy By Heather Taylor

I have told you this so that my joy may be in you and that your joy may be complete. ~ *John 15: 11 (NIV)*

Did you know that joy is not just, well, enjoyable but it is God's desire for us to have complete joy? Our Father has designed us perfectly and even our emotions are created to help us live an extraordinary life. I realize it may be hard to see how John 15:11 fits into finding and claiming my identity, but I promise it does.

For a very long time, I had the misconception of thinking if something brought me joy it could not be benefitting God. Crazy, I know that now, but I spent a very long time believing that. Imagine trying to find your calling, but every time you did what God called you to do, and you enjoyed it, you thought that meant it couldn't be from God, so it must be your flesh. That was me. I loved to write and speak. It brought me so much pleasure. If I could make someone laugh, then I was ecstatic, which of course was a clear sign that it couldn't be from God! I prayed for God to reveal my calling, but He never did. Ironically, at the same time, I was praying for revelation, I started getting opportunities to speak and write. I would get excited and often thought, "this must be God!" Once the engagement was over, I would realize I enjoyed it too much, so it couldn't be from Him. I believed for a task to be your calling, you had to be unhappy (or at least not be completely elated). I couldn't be doing God's work if I was feeling all this joy.

During a Bible study, I read John 15:11, and it set me free! When I read, "I have told you this so that my joy may be in you," everything came together in an instant! God had once again found a way to penetrate my stubborn brain and take my legalistic beliefs and disprove them. Our Father is like all fathers: He wants us to have joy and to have it completely. Why would He give us a task and not make it enjoyable for us? I grew in my identity that day by claiming what was mine all along: joy in my calling.

Lord Jesus, I ask you to fill me with true and perfect joy—the joy You promised us and long for us to have. I pray that even in the darkest night and in the midst of the strongest storm I can be filled with a joy that is unshakable and so clearly supernatural. Amen.

I am Joyful

picture

How would it feel to receive the kind of joy that Jesus speaks of in John 15:11?

ask

Do you have joy in your heart even when things are going bad? Why or why not?

pray

My Father, My Friend By Amy Oaks

I no longer call you servants, because a servant does not know his master's business. Instead, I have called you friends, for everything that I learned from my Father I have made known to you.
~ John 15:15 (NIV)

I am the oldest of four children, while my husband is an only child. We joke that he doesn't share well, and I can be a bit of a mother hen. My brothers, sister, and I are all four years apart from one another, which means my younger sister was only six years old when I went off to college. My next oldest brother was in high school and my other brother was in middle school. What were my parents thinking? I missed a lot of their growing up during those years, and still feel twinges of guilt about abandoning them. I moved out, went to college, worked during the summers, and married only a year after graduating. My family went through a tumultuous time then, so it was easier to step away from that situation and start my own life.

Today, my siblings and I are all friends; married with children, so we have plenty of common ground on which to connect. We can look back on our upbringing now and laugh about both the good times and the bad. We realize that relationships ebb and flow. People go through times of growth or change and sometimes need a break from a relationship as part of those phases. Other times, we need each other more than ever. No matter what season we find ourselves in, God assures us we can always pick up where we left off.

God, my loving Father, is like that too. He will never abandon me, though I distance myself from Him sometimes. In John 15:15, Jesus called His disciples His friends, as He was open and honest with them about His life and lessons. My Father always walks alongside me. Sometimes we walk in silence. Sometimes I do all the talking. Our most impactful times together are when I take the time to listen—really listen— to Him. It means being intentional and patient so I can hear and understand what He's trying to teach me. It means being present, especially when it's hard! For that's what true friendship is all about.

Dear Lord, thank you for the gift of Your friendship, loyalty, love, and everlasting wisdom. Guide me to live a life that keeps our friendship strong. In Your Name I pray, Amen.

I am the Father's Friend

picture

What can you do to keep lines of communication open, and your friendship with God your Father strong?

ask

Who can you count on in this world when life gets hard?

pray

With Confidence By Luanne Nelson

I will remain in the world no longer, but they are still in the world, and I am coming to you. Holy Father, protect them by the power of your name, the name you gave me, so that they may be one as we are one ~ John 17:11 (NIV)

Christ offered this scriptural prayer for His people alone as believers; not for the world at large. We can go to God our Father with confidence because our Savior is right there with us! He is our Holy Protector. We do not battle the enemy alone. We have the strength and the might of His holy power in every step we take. There is no reason for fear. There is no reason for trepidation.

Have you ever shooed away the evil one simply by saying, "I am saved by the most precious blood of Jesus"? Do it! The devil shrivels and flees instantly. Have you ever prayed with one of God's children – our brothers and sisters in Jesus Christ - for His powerful healing? Do it! He is with us to alleviate our suffering. All glory is His! Have you ever asked Him for direction and listened carefully for His answer? Do it! He is right here with us! Reading and meditating on His powerful love letters to us in His Word deepens our relationship with Him. My life changed the moment I accepted Him as my Lord and Savior! Yours will, too. He is not "up there or over there." He is not an absentee parent; He is present right here with us right now in His Holy Spirit!

"If He is for us, who can be against us?" (Romans 8:31 NIV) "No weapon that is formed against you will prosper; And every tongue that accuses you in judgment you will condemn. This is the heritage of the servants of the Lord, And their vindication is from Me, declares the Lord." (Isaiah 54:17 NASB) "Do not touch My anointed ones; do my prophets no harm." (Psalm 105:15 NIV)

Jesus says, "They are not of the world, even as I am not of it. Sanctify them by the truth; your word is truth. As You sent me into the world, I have sent them into the world." (John 17:16-18 NIV)

Dear Holy God Almighty, Thank You for not leaving us here alone weaponless against the devil. We know the battle is real. Thank You for Your Holy weapons! Thank You for the power in Your Holy Name! Amen.

I am a Warrior

picture

When do I find the most joy in rendering the enemy weaponless, thanking Father God Almighty for this Power through Him?

ask

How do you ask Him to cover you with His protection and give you grace every day? Do you read His Word to deepen your relationship with Him? How do you share the knowledge of the Power in His Name with your brothers and sisters in Him?

pray

I am a Warrior

No Longer That Way By Joni Jones

But God demonstrates His own love for us in this: While we were still sinners, Christ died for us.
~ Romans 5:8 (NIV)

She's always been that way. She will never change. It will take a miracle. Have you ever said or thought this? You may eat your words, because the worst of the worst, Paul, the one who penned the words "of whom I am the worst" (1 Timothy 1:15), he was that way. A forgotten detail that changes everything about his story, making his story our story. How blind I am at times forgetting a detail, a very important detail, that changes everything.

Paul was the worst of the worst. He persecuted the followers of Jesus, yet he tells us to "put into practice whatever he learned, received, heard seen in him" (Philippians 4:9). The worst of the worst asks us to follow his lead? Yes, but it is what he did after he experienced the risen Lord, the One who took over his mind, heart, and soul. The One who stopped him in his worst, physically blinding him in the midst of his being spiritually blind. The One who told Saul he did not have to clean up his act before he met Jesus, because he needed Jesus to clean up his act. A new name and a new identity, Saul to Paul in Him.

Paul is us. I am the worst of the worst, yet I have experienced the power of the risen One. I was blind, but now I see the risen One who enables me to put into practice all that I have learned, received, heard and seen from Paul. We, too, can live as one of Jesus' followers, by walking as one who is no longer seen as the worst in God's eyes, because "while we were still sinners Christ died for us." (Romans 5:8)

Whenever you delay going to Jesus because you feel like the worst of the worst, instead run into His arms. Jesus died for Paul, the worst of the worst. Now, Paul will always be that way because he followed the One who is the Way. If Paul can do it, we can do it, so that we will always be this way, in Him.

Dear Lord, how can I ever say thank You enough for loving me and dying for me, even when I was that way. Thank You that I don't have to bring you anything because You have done it all for me on the cross. Amen.

I am Redeemed

picture

How does the truth that Paul, who was the worst of the worst, received God's favor help you to receive God's favor, especially in your not good enough moments?

ask

In what area of your life do you need to take a step of faith and live as accepted and redeemed by God?

pray

Dead to the World By Luanne Nelson

We have therefore been buried with Him through baptism into death so that just as Christ was raised from the dead through the glory and power of the Father, we too might walk habitually in newness of life abandoning our old ways. ~ Romans 6:4 (AMP)

A red scruffy beard covered his crooked smile, his eyes gave him away. He seemed to have a strange understanding of the universe which was confirmed when he said, "I am dead to the world." I had to look away. He wore a long black robe and old, weathered shoes. I thought he was a monk but learned later he was an abbot. Passing through town, he had stayed with us overnight. In the morning, I offered him a plate of pancakes. He said, "No, thank you, I have to leave now." His eyes twinkled. We said our good-byes. His words about being dead stayed with me. How could someone so sparkly be dead? It took me a long time to figure out what he meant. Finally, I found the answer in Romans 6:4, "We have therefore been buried with Him through baptism into death so that just as Christ was raised from the dead through the glory and power of the Father, we too might walk habitually in newness of life abandoning our old ways."

I've come to realize, we are not only baptized as Jesus Christ was baptized, but we are crucified and die with Him, too, at our baptism. Jesus paid the debt for our sins through His death; we die to this world the moment we become His. We make a decision to walk away from our earthly flesh, from our worldly way of life. We die to this world the moment we commit ourselves to Him. We become part of the Spiritual Body of Christ. When He was raised in victory over sin and death, we were raised, too. This does not mean that as His disciples we do not sin, or that we won't be tempted. Rather, we strive to become dead to the flesh, dead to the world, to be fully alive in Jesus Christ. We are changed. We say, "No, I am not doing that anymore." Becoming a disciple of Jesus means burning our bridges to our past life of sin. Being baptized in Him rids us of our old life, our old ways. We become dead to the world and new Creations in Him.

Oh, dear Jesus, Lord God Almighty, raise me up! Raise me from the dead! Raise me from the depths of my own desperation! Thank you for the blessed opportunity to start over again in You. Make me Your new creation. Please make me dead to this world and alive in You! Amen.

I am a New Creation

picture

What specific aspect of the old life do you need to cast off so that you can now walk in newness of life?

ask

How is the enemy playing mind games with us when we say, "I'm dead to sin" when at times we feel very much alive to it? What does God's Word say is the truth about this?

pray

I am a New Creation

Servant of God By Luanne Nelson

What benefit did you reap at that time from the things you are now ashamed of? Those things result in death! But now that you have been set free from sin and have become slaves of God, the benefit you reap leads to holiness, and the result is eternal life. For the wages of sin is death, but the gift of God is eternal life in Christ Jesus our LORD. ~ Romans 6:21-23 (NASB)

God is not the King of convenience. He is not Lord of easy street, and He certainly is not the Creator of the cheat sheet and cutting corners. Sister Naomi tried to teach us this in the fourth grade. I listened to her, sitting on my wooden chair while carefully lifting my desktop just enough to grab an M&M my mom had tucked into my lunch bag. A childhood punctuated with little white lies, sneaking candy, cutting corners, doing chores and throwing temper tantrums were slippery slopes into bigger sins, she said.

She taught us a little jingle with the words, "Give food to the hungry, drink to the thirsty, clothe the naked, visit the imprisoned, shelter the homeless, visit the sick and bury the dead." She told us to remember this song when we were "near the occasion of sin" and do one of them. She was teaching us the corporal works of mercy as taught by Jesus from His sermon on the Mount! In retrospect, I learned everything I needed to know to navigate this life into holy waters from her. Thinking about it decades later, had I simply tucked away my bookbag on the last day of fourth grade and followed her directions, I really didn't need to have any further formal education.

I am not going to list my sins here. The list is long and I am guessing yours is, too. Christ came to save everyone: even the perfect kids, the smartest ones, the kids on death row in prison. Every single one of us. No exceptions. In reaching that point where we've had enough of ourselves, we become His "slaves." Instead of slaves to sin, we produce the fruit of holiness rather than gathering the dead thistles of shame and death. In the end, God has promised us everlasting life. The decision is ours to make. Which fruit would we rather have, shame and death or holiness and life?

Sister Naomi was right. It was a slippery slope. I nearly totaled my life careening out of control. Today, I strive to be a servant of God rather than a slave to sin. I am grateful to her. I am His.

God, Your way is so much better, Lord God Almighty. Thank You for the loving teachers You put in my life, thank You for my Dad and Mom who spent so much time and money on me, never giving up on me. It wasn't wasted after all. Amen.

I am Free from Sin

picture

What does the concept of "free will" mean to you? What defines your life?

ask

What is the difference between a slave and a servant? Why should we split hairs over these secular definitions?

pray

Flawless By Joni Jones

Therefore, there is now no condemnation for those who are in Christ Jesus. ~ Romans 8:1 (NIV)

I lived my life seeking perfection because I believed that if I was seen as perfect then I would be loved perfectly. Perfection, performance-based living ... always seeking yet never receiving. I looked up into the eyes of the Perfect One in the midst of the mess I have made through my quest and heard the one word that changed everything: forgiven.

No judgment, no disapproval, no reprimand, as I live in Him, "for those who are in Christ Jesus." The verdict is "Not Guilty," making us His precious child who is perfect in Him. Perfect, without blemish, covered by the perfect One who overlooks all our imperfections. Believing there is no condemnation is what enables us to live as flawless. Oh, flawless one, we are covered by the perfection that lives beyond the mirror, because perfection isn't looking, feeling, and being perfect. It is being forgiven perfectly for being imperfect. And we can't do it on our own, no matter how hard we try. In Jesus, there is no condemnation, so living in perfection becomes our reality only in Him.

Flawless is not looking, feeling, or being perfect. Flawless is being perfectly loved by God. Flawless is being perfectly imperfect in His perfection. Flawless is who we become when we accept all who God says we are, despite our flaws. Flawless is receiving and believing that you are fearfully and wonderfully made as God's workmanship. Flawless makes you His daughter. Flawless is receiving and believing that you are loved by the Father, redeemed by His Son, and the Holy Spirit living you who gives you the power to live beyond your flaws. Flawless because Jesus does not condemn.

Amazing grace how sweet the sound that took a perfectly flawed woman like me and loved me back together piece by piece, with His peace. His peace covers us with His perfection, so today we live as flawless. Only Jesus takes away the not from our every feeling or believing we are not enough, For there is no condemnation making us perfectly imperfect in Him. Believe it. Receive it. Live it.

Lord, I am amazed that you have made a way for there to be no more condemnation for my sin. Thank You for Jesus. Thank You that you call me flawless because of the sacrifice that was made. Amen.

I am Flawless

picture

How does the truth that in Christ you are flawless to God, replace condemnation in your life?

ask

What does your life look like without condemnation? How would you be different?

pray

I am Flawless

Trust in ME By Michelle Meade

For all who are led by The Spirit of God are sons of God. ~ Romans 8:14 (ESV)

Ask any parent of an abused orphan the insurmountable task of teaching trust. You will weep with them the way God lamented over the children of Israel. God shows He is trustworthy by the way He leads, feeds, and meets our needs. He grieves when we want to live the Burger King slogan and "have it our way." But He doesn't grieve because of us; He grieves over us. And if we let Him, He will wipe our tears and grieve with us.

It took many hard tumbles riddled with spiritual "road rash" to learn this truth. There was one particular fall, so epic, I feared I'd never recover. God knew otherwise. He faithfully led me and fed me until I could stand again. His first instruction in this restoration process was to stay and soak in Hebrews chapter 12 for seven months! The first half of the chapter unveils the triumphant overcomer, while the second half reveals how we overcome. God's answer is entirely immersed in the process of training. In my amplified Bible, it mentions some form of the word discipline over 20 times! When we resist His counsel, refuse to agree with Truth, and maintain a justified response, the fruit will be a hardened orphan heart left pained by the marks of His rod. However, if we choose to be trained, we will respond with humility and repentance and live satiated as sons in the peaceable fruit of righteousness. Then, those training marks will be precious evidence of God's Fatherhood.

Through submission to God's discipline, our identity is disclosed. May we reach for His Hand in trust to guide.

'do not doubt, do not fear - for your God I AM is here
Trust in ME, on My Name call - I'll keep your foot so you won't fall
I'll strengthen, help, and hold your hand - Trust In ME and you shall stand.
I know the way, wait and see - it shall unfold as you Trust in ME'
Copyright 2007 Remember MEmore.com

Abba Daddy, I repent for pulling away from your loving correction.
I desire to see you undo every work of darkness in my life and
make all things new. Amen.

I am Moldable

picture

When you turn from self and Trust in God, every torn thread of your life is woven into a beautiful tapestry.

ask

Have you seen God turn your "mess" into His "message?" What story does your tapestry display?

pray

I am Moldable

A Cup of Grace By Lisa Danegelis

For you did not receive the spirit of bondage again to fear, but you received the spirit of adoption by whom we cry out Abba, Father. ~ Romans 8:15 (NKJV)

Has God ever bought you a coffee? He just gave me one! We made it together in my kitchen; a triple shot white mocha to be exact, at 6 AM. He stopped me in the middle of writing for this very book! He also stopped me in the middle of a restrictive sugar detox and a fast! He knew I needed to drink from His deep well of grace. I'm sipping it with Him right now. It is so fun! God and I made a mocha together! I glance out my window at a brilliant orange sunrise and the tears flow. As I feel His Spirit wash over me I thank Him with a giddiness of heart that can be foreign to me. I am still learning - always learning - about His never-ending supply of grace. I nestle back into the sofa and His words start to flow:

"My grace is so complete. So consuming. So bountiful. So embracing. It chases you when you run and patiently waits as you hide. It encourages you when you stumble and forgives you when you fall. It covers your frustration and questions, and the chaos and confusion, your little slip-ups and monumental failures. Your days of anger, resentment and envy, and yes, even your times of disobedience. I can handle your deepest pain and wildest rage. I can handle your days of silence and months of complacency. Even years of distance and rebellion cannot quench My passionate pursuit."

As always, His words leave me undone. Sometimes we may look at God as a taskmaster keeping score. Romans 8:15 states the opposite. "Abba Father" is an endearing term and emphasizes the intimacy of His Fatherhood. There is no bondage in this relationship, only deep love, and acceptance. God desires that we experience His grace in every broken empty place of our soul. Our lives need to be bathed in it. It is a gift beyond comprehension and without measure. There is nothing we can do to earn it and there is no way to pay Him back. After all, that is what a gift from the heart of love is all about anyway, isn't it?

I'm finished writing and my coffee cup is still half full. I don't really want it anymore ... it was His gift to you; a cup of grace, from His heart, through my pen.

May my relationship with You be bathed in Your grace, Father. Help me to be a humble recipient of Your lavish supply. Amen.

I am Bathed in Grace

picture

How would your life look different if you completely believed His love for you? How can you cultivate these changes today, next week, next year?

ask

What is hard to believe about God's grace? What is freeing about God's grace? What is exhilarating about God's grace?

pray

I am Bathed in Grace

God Loves Us as Much as He Loves Jesus By Marlene Dawson

And if we are [His] children, then we are His heirs also: heirs of God and fellow heirs with Christ [sharing His inheritance with Him]; only we must also share His suffering if we are to share His glory. ~ Romans 8:17 (AMPC)

Belonging. We all need to belong somewhere: a family, a group of friends, a club. I read this verse many times before I understood it means that I am a joint heir with Jesus. Whenever I thought about being an heir with Jesus I only saw my failures and flaws. But God's word tells me because I asked Jesus into my heart, I am God's daughter and Jesus' fellow heir. "What does fellow heir mean, exactly, Lord?" I asked God after thinking about it for months. His answer took me from fear and doubt to knowing I would eventually become free from the pain of horrible childhood abuse, perpetrated by my biological dad, among others. God said, "Being a joint heir with Jesus means I love you as much as I love Him!" WOW, GOD!

Have you ever expected an inheritance? Well, we get to share in the inheritance of Jesus! This means all He inherits, we inherit. We get to share in His suffering, yes, but not His crucifixion for all of our sins; that was Christ's alone. The Bible says that since the world hated Jesus, it will hate us, too. We don't like hearing this one very much; our tendency is working to make sure everyone likes us. Our culture is so focused on being liked that we even count how many people "like" us on social media. This is not what makes us children of God. Asking Jesus to forgive our sins and come live in our hearts is how we are made new in Christ, or born again, and fellow heirs with Jesus. We must want to have this personal relationship with God. It will keep us for a lifetime on earth, and then forever in eternity. There are a few life-changing steps to become born again.

First, we must say that Jesus is Lord, and then believe that God (the Father) raised Jesus (the Son) from the dead. Next, we admit we are sinners, ask God to forgive us, and invite Jesus to live in our hearts. Then get a Bible and begin reading it. Find a group of people who support your new faith in God, who believe what the Bible says, and encourages you to grow in faith.

Dear God, I believe Jesus is Lord; I believe you raised Him from the dead. I know I'm a sinner, please forgive me. Jesus, please come live in my heart and be my Lord and Savior. Thank You. Amen.

I am a Co-Heir with Jesus

picture

Share your experience of becoming a child of God. If you have not asked to be God's child yet, why not today? Pray the prayer at the bottom of the previous page, then write about your experience.

ask

What would be an example in your life of being a fellow heir with Christ?

pray

I am a Co-Heir with Jesus

All Things By Luanne Nelson

And we know that in all things God works for the good of those who love him, who have been called according to his purpose. ~ Romans 8:28 (NIV)

He looked straight at me, completely emotionless, and asked, "Are you sick or are you fat because you eat too much?" A few months later, I saw him again and told him he was the rudest person I'd met in a long time. He flatly responded saying, "You know, all things work together for the Glory of God and the good of mankind." I wanted to punch him in the nose both times. I didn't, though. I had no desire to get arrested and thrown in jail because of this idiot. Clearly, in retrospect, grace was at work, too.

Often, people issue platitudes referencing this verse to make the other person feel better - or worse! It comes off sounding like spiritual sloth. "Don't sweat it, it will work out for the good of all" or, "I can say whatever I want, I am important at Church." People who are suffering are never helped by flippancy or by a holier than thou attitude. The sufferer will dismiss such counsel as nonsense and dismiss the spiritual caregiver ... bringing me back to this: Absolutely nothing good is going to happen after telling a woman she's fat. The keywords in this verse are: "who have been called according to His purpose." This call is two-fold. First, we must respond to God's grace, His calling, His gift of Christ and the Holy Spirit, His gift of revealing knowledge and understanding of what is happening. Second, we must accept His invitation to be one of the ones "called according to His purpose." This does not mean just receiving the invitation, it means opening the invitation, responding to it, and saying "yes."

So, you see, not punching that guy in the nose was a good thing for him - and for me, too. Walking in grace is hard sometimes. Remembering to display spiritual manners can be tough. I often have to remind myself that God loves all His kids - even the ones who have fallen away from Him as I did years ago. He brought me back to Him, and it's in prayer and grace that I can be a walking example of His love and grace - bringing others back to Him, too.

Thank you, Father God Almighty, for sending out invitations to serve You and patiently waiting for us to open them! All Glory and Honor to You always and forever. Amen.

I am Called

picture

How do you exercise your spirituality to be in great shape for those sticky spiritual moments?

ask

What do you do when you recognize opportunities to make lemonade out of lemons when they're thrown our way?

pray

I am Called

Triumph Over Every Trouble By Sue Sherstad

Yet even in the midst of all these things, we triumph over them all, for God has made us to be more than conquerors, and His demonstrated love is our glorious victory over everything! ~ Romans 8:37 (TPT)

You are a winner! You have within you all that you need to triumph over every trouble or problem that you will ever face. I know that because God declares it in His word about us. Paul says, "God has made us to be more than conquerors." In the Greek, more is "Huper", meaning over, above, and beyond. It is the idea of superiority—greater, unequaled, and unrivaled by any person or thing. The word conqueror in the Greek is "Nikos". This describes an overcomer, champion, victor or master depicting an overwhelming, prevailing force. When these two words are combined we have "Hupernikos", which declares you are an overwhelming conqueror, an enormous overcomer. That's who you are in Jesus Christ! Never think or talk about yourself as anything less. As a new creation in Christ and filled with the Holy Spirit you are made to be more than a conqueror. His love has empowered you to be unrivaled, more than enough to face any foe.

I had the most amazing encounter with the Lord one day. I had the habit of going to a park for my lunch break. I found a secluded place and sat on a picnic table on a beautiful summer day. I was praying when suddenly a monarch butterfly landed on my hand. I became very still and the Lord began to speak to me. He told me of His great love for me and that He saw the struggles, doubts, and fears. He reassured me that I belonged to Him and as this butterfly was resting in my hand, He was holding me in His Hand calling me to trust Him. I sensed His overwhelming presence as He reminded me that nothing can separate me from His love. The butterfly remained on my hand for over 20 minutes. As I left I sensed the power of His presence going with me knowing everything was going to be alright. Whenever I face troubles or the pressures of life, I remember the butterfly and what the Lord spoke to me. I have confidence in His Love and His power to triumph over everything! He loves you and has given you the power to be triumphant!

Lord, I believe that You have made me more than a conqueror and that I am triumphant! I put my trust in your love and power for "a glorious hyper-victory!" In Jesus' Name! Amen.

I am Triumphant

picture

How will this passage affect the way you respond the next time you face adversity?

ask

What did you learn about being an overcomer in Christ from this verse?

pray

I am Triumphant

Nothing Separates Us By Noreen Lessmann

For I am convinced that neither death nor life, neither angels nor demons, neither the present nor the future, nor any powers, neither height nor depth nor anything else in all creation, will be able to separate us from the love of God that is in Christ Jesus Our Lord. ~ Romans 8:38-39 (NIV)

Nothing can separate us from God 's love; nothing. Absolutely nothing, not one thing. This verse tenderly embraces me with reassurance. I have lost family members, friends, acquaintances and co-workers of whom I held in high esteem and dearly loved. These words were used in their celebration of life services and remained ingrained in me. It is indeed a consolation and comfort to know that we are inseparable from the love of God—that white, hot radiant and permeating love of God that is in Christ Jesus.

Life is fraught with very hard difficulty that we are not immune to suffering. In the midst of despair, where we can barely cry out, "God help me," it is imperative that we hold onto Christ and lean into Him to pull through the devastating season of life that we find ourselves. As we hide these verses in our hearts and revisit them frequently, they will sustain us and remind us of who we are and whose we are in Christ. We are more than conquerors. As we transition through life cycles and progress through suffering and grief, Christ will sustain us with His love. Though we are grieved, we are loved. Though we have lost, we are loved. Though we can barely cry out, we are loved. We are reassured of His love.

Oh, Most Heavenly God, wrap me in Your love. Lift me up and sustain me. In You, I am reassured and I decide to trust, knowing that nothing will separate me from the love of God that is in Christ Jesus, My Lord.

I am Reassured

picture

How can trusting in God's love in the midst of difficulty be put into practice? How will this passage affect your ability to pass through life's trouble?

ask

How does God sustain you in times of difficulty and despair?

pray

I am Reassured

All We Need By Lisa Danegelis

For in Him and to Him and through Him are all things, to whom be glory forever.
~ Romans 11:36 (NKJV)

My life was in chaos. Five children ages ten to eighteen, a high profile catering business that needed my attention and escalating health issues were taking their toll. I felt like the very last bit of life was being sucked from my tattered soul. I was desperately looking for comfort, reprieve, something, anything. As often happens when I am bustling about in a flurry of mental, emotional and physical exhaustion and confusion, God stops me in mid-gait and gives me a word! I literally have to run for a pen and paper. He knew I needed to reconnect with my Source of Life, the Answer to all my needs, my First Love. His wisdom flowed from my pen:

"As you search for others, you will find it is Me. As you look to busyness, you will find it is Me.

As you crave peace, I will be there. As you seek wild-eyed for the solace, the answer, the unmet need, you will find it is Me. Nothing on this earth will satisfy like Me, nothing. I will fill the void as you seek Me. Your peace will not come from your family, more friends, a more organized life, only from Me. I need those on the front lines who hold their peace, who are stable, untethered, unfazed by this life. I need you to find this peace in Me. It is so deep, so real, so unconditional, so special, so precious, so lasting, so restful, so magical. Peace in all things, all relationships, all situations; unshakeable, unthinkable peace, is yours ... in Me!"

My scattered brain and restless soul breathed a sigh of relief. He is all I need, I am complete in Him. Evangelist Graham Cooke describes the beauty of a life completely abandoned to our Creator: "I have been to hell and prospered because He held my hand. I have lost everything and thrived. I have been in the valley of the shadow and lost all fear. I have been on the mountain bathed in a light so strong I thought I would dissolve in happiness." Aren't Graham's words breathtaking? May we all know our God so intimately and be able to declare, "You are all we need!"

Consume me, Father. I want to know You as my All! Amen.

I am at Peace

picture

How would your life look different if you knew Jesus was your All-in-All?

ask

What do trick yourself into thinking you need most often? How do these false beliefs come out in your life?

pray

Yielding To The Will of God By Sue Sherstad

Beloved friends, what should be our proper response to God's marvelous mercies? I encourage you to surrender yourselves to God to be His sacred, living sacrifices. And live in holiness, experiencing all that delights His heart. For this becomes your genuine expression of worship. Stop imitating the ideals and opinions of the culture around you, but be inwardly transformed by the Holy Spirit through a total reformation of how you think. This will empower you to discern God's will as you live a beautiful life, satisfying and perfect in His eyes. ~ Romans 12:1-2 (TPT)

I've found that when I surrender myself to the Lordship of Jesus, His ways and plans are always so much better than what I wanted. I've learned to yield to and obey the Holy Spirit, from letting go of wrong relationships to being quick to obey the Spirit's correction to forgive. Being conformed into the image of Jesus and living out His plan requires submission to Him. The Apostle Paul was encouraging the believers to offer themselves as a living sacrifice in light of the marvelous mercies of God. So, what does it mean to be a living sacrifice? It's not lying down on the altar like the old covenant animal sacrifices. Jesus is asking that we give Him everything about our lives. Sacrifice is "anything consecrated and offered to God." As His children, our response to the mercies of God should be one of total surrender to our Lord Jesus Christ. He gave it all for you, bought you with His blood. You belong to Him, your life is not your own.

When you begin to live your life surrendered completely to Jesus, a beautiful transformation takes place from the inside out. You will check your heart motives for why you are doing what you are doing. Yielding to Jesus means not holding on to that grudge or remaining upset and angry at the people in your life. It's letting go of your rights and learning to submit to the leading of the Holy Spirit. It's called dying to self. I know it sounds painful—it is. The flesh doesn't want to die. But to truly live the abundant life and experience true freedom, we must yield to the will of God for our lives. Paul said, "I have been crucified with Christ; it is no longer I who live, but Christ lives in me; and the life I now live in the body I live by faith in the Son of God, Who loved me and gave Himself up for me. (Galatians 2:20)

Your genuine expression of worship is living a life devoted to Jesus, a life that pleases Him in your actions, thoughts, and service to Him. There is no greater reward than living a holy life, set apart for Him. A yielded life is the only life worth living. A beautiful life that Glorifies Jesus!

Lord Jesus, I thank you for your mercy in my life. I yield to You and surrender myself to You as a living sacrifice to live the beautiful life that You have planned for me. Amen.

I am Yielded

picture

What is the Holy Spirit asking you to do in obedience to this scripture?

ask

What does it mean to be a living sacrifice unto God?

pray

I am Yielded

The Test By Heather Taylor

Do not repay anyone evil for evil. Be careful to do what is right in the eyes of everyone. If it is possible, as far as it depends on you, live at peace with everyone. Do not take revenge, my dear friends but leave room for God's wrath, for it is written; "It is mine to avenge; I will repay says the Lord."
~ Romans 12:17-19 (NIV)

Claiming our identity in Christ isn't a one-and-done deal. We have to continue to make the right choices as we walk out our destiny. Mistakes will be made and backsliding can happen, but it is beautiful that during these times God never leaves us how we are. Forgiveness is a hard lesson I've had to learn over and over again. I know the truth and I know that I am often the only obstacle in my own way.

Paul urged the believers not to take revenge but to allow God to avenge us. Not delivering the "wrath of Heather" on my enemies has not been the easiest lesson for me to learn. Just like learning to forgive, I had to learn to love my enemy, allowing God to deal with their sins against me. Not an easy task at all! We have all been hurt by someone. Most have been disappointed by several 'someones' but maybe you're like me and there's that one person in particular that has crushed you so bad, that their actions have permanently changed a piece of you forever. In my case, that person showed absolutely no remorse for the pain she caused. I spent a lot of time filled with hate and probably a longer time wishing harm on her. In the end, I didn't feel any better and she didn't feel anything at all.

I finally got on the floor and begged God to help me—I was a mess. I had lost so much of myself because of hate and hurt. I needed help and God was the only one who could cure me. Revenge is not satisfying in the end; I knew that deep down. But my heart was blinded by my wounds. I needed to repent for the hate I felt toward her. God helped me, like He always does, to let go of my need to be the punisher. True to His Word, He did deal with her sin, but because He rescued me and changed my heart, I wasn't relieved or happy about it. I felt sad for her. Once again, God removed another piece of the old me and etched in the new and improved me, the woman He designed me to be; a woman that could have mercy on her enemy and not take revenge.

Father, forgive the people in my life that have betrayed me, lied to me, mistreated me, or used me. Have mercy on them so that they will see Your love and fall repentant at your feet. Amen.

I am Merciful

picture

What would it feel like to release that anger and give it to God?

ask

Can you relate to my story above about wanting revenge and feeling no mercy? How?

pray

I am Merciful

You Already Have It By Susan Brozek

Accept one another, then, just as Christ accepted you, in order to bring praise to God.
~ Romans 15:7 (NIV)

One of the most important needs we have as human beings is to know that we are accepted. The need for acceptance is so strong that at times, we will go to great lengths to find it. So often we stand in judgment of others when what each of us actually needs is just to be accepted for who we are. When we desire to be accepted by another person or a group, we place ourselves in a somewhat vulnerable position, because their acceptance of us can take on an elevated level of importance such that if we are rejected, it can feel devastating. In contrast, Christ met people right where they were. He didn't expect them to have their act together when they encountered Him. Jesus merely accepted people unconditionally, holding out His loving hand to pull them to Himself.

For human beings though, this type of pure and unconditional acceptance of others is very elusive. No person can demonstrate it perfectly, and because of this, many people get hurt and take offense, searching for other avenues of acceptance and ways to fit in, no matter how unhealthy those options might be. In addition, some people, when fearing or expecting rejection, will go so far as to sabotage a relationship before the other party has a chance to reject them first. In my Christian psychotherapy practice, I call this "preemptive rejection." In other words, it is making a choice to reject someone else before they can reject you because it won't seem as painful. This is an example of our desire to self-protect instead of letting God do it for us, and it accomplishes nothing but the building of walls around our hearts.

The best and first place to seek acceptance is to go to God. As is stated in Romans 15:7, we already have it! The very things we search for in this world are already provided for us by the One who is intimately acquainted with all our deepest needs. Knowing and living out the truth that we are accepted by God and this is our true identity in Christ can be the solid rock beneath our feet to see ourselves as fully accepted in Him! Stop living for acceptance...you already have it from the One who matters most.

Lord, thank You for Your complete acceptance. Help me allow this knowledge to move from my head to my heart. God, help me to know that You accept me no matter what and I belong to You (John 17:19)! Amen.

I am Accepted

picture

Identity a season in your life where you could sense God's loving acceptance of you when you felt rejected by another person or a group of people.

ask

How would your life be different if you truly embraced, on every level, the fact that you are totally accepted by God?

pray

I am Accepted

Bound for Heaven's Shore By Lisa Danegelis

Eye has not seen, nor ear heard, nor has entered into the hearts of man the things which God has prepared for those who love Him. ~ 1 Corinthians 2:9 (NKJV)

"I am good! I am good! I am good!

I am your next breath and heartbeat. I created that strawberry you are admiring and the chocolate you are dipping it in! I thought so deeply and carefully as I created the tastes, textures, sounds and subtle nuances of life. I designed the colors to meld together into tapestries woven in the sky (my favorite is a pink and orange sunset with a brush of purple!). I considered the shades and textures of green when My Hand swept across the prairies and forests. My breath brought forth incredible forms of life! I had so much fun making giraffes, turtles and quirky little bugs! I thought of everything! For you!

The tender flower petals and granite rocks declare my personality! Yes - I have a personality! I am soft and gentle and solid and immovable, merciful and long-suffering, steady and sure. My Hand can shade a lily of the valley and command a violent wind. I am in all and overall ... I AM All. I laughed when I created wiggly baby toes and was delighted when I decided on red hair! I have such love for you, My children, my heart could explode! Do you know there is not one laugh in the whole world that is the same? I love to laugh! Laugh with Me, My precious ones! Look around at the incredible beauty of life and rejoice with Me! It's all for you! The snowy mountain cap and beautiful coral. The feeling of a thousand grains of sand between your toes and the gentle breeze caressing your face. The snowflakes that dance in a million patterns and the mist mysteriously enrobing the lowlands! Embrace it all and rejoice! You live in a glorious art studio!"

These precious words from the heart of our extravagant God give me Holy Spirit chills! He stopped me at work while I was dipping strawberries to tell me about His glorious creation. I felt His excitement! The beauty and mystery of this world are just a taste of what our Creator has waiting for us in Heaven. I can envision Him waiting with excitement to unveil His Heavenly Kingdom to us. The magnificence will be beyond our wildest dreams! I can't wait!

Creator God, thank you for the beauty that surrounds me! May my anticipation of Your extravagance only grow as I wait for my heavenly home. Amen.

I am Bound for Heaven

picture

Did you know God is preparing treasures for you in Heaven today? How can you take time to be grateful for these good gifts He storing up for you? What do you think they are?

ask

What seemingly insignificant blessings are you grateful for today?

pray

I am Bound for Heaven

My Favorite Body Part By Traci Weldie

Do you not know that you are God's temple and that God's Spirit dwells in you?
~ I Corinthians 3:16 (NLT)

We are all familiar with the teaching that as believers, we all play a role in the body of the Church. So, what's your favorite body part? I think I am partial to the eyes; I definitely am grateful to be able to look around and see God's beautiful creation. But wait, I think my favorite might be the ear; after all, I am that woman lifting my hands to God praising Him when I hear a beautiful song. Oh, so is my favorite body part my arms? What if I couldn't lift them? And what if I couldn't stand? So, maybe my favorite body part is the leg. But if I didn't have a brain ... or a heart ... or a liver ... or lungs? How can I possibly choose a favorite body part? That is exactly why Paul describes the Church as a body with many parts. The body needs all its parts in order to function, just as the Church must have all its parts to function. There is no need to pick a favorite one, or for that matter believe that one part is more important than another.

Paul goes on, in Ephesians, to call us God's temple. The temple in the Old Testament represented the place where God would dwell. With the resurrection of Christ and the sending of the Holy Spirit, WE are the temple where the Holy Spirit dwells. It's important to note that the "you" in this verse is actually plural and that means WE are the temple. All of us as believers. The feet. The eyes. Even the pancreas and gallbladder (not sure who THAT would be!). So, when we gather as the Church, we should be making it evident and palpable that the Holy Spirit is present, dwelling in us.

As the temple and body of Christ, we must resist the temptation to elevate certain parts over others and understand that a beautiful, attention-getting EYE would not function without the spleen doing its job daily. As the BODY, where the Holy Spirit dwells, we need to look different than the world and celebrate every KNEECAP and PINKY TOE and SMALL INTESTINE!

Dear Lord, thank You for how You perfectly created me to play a role in the body of believers. Help me to recognize, accept and then thrive in the role You want me to fill. Amen.

I am Part of His Body

picture

What is your role in the Church? Have you ever found yourself longing to fulfill a different role? Why?

ask

How will you best fulfill the role God wants you to fill in the Church?

pray

Messes By Heidi Sampson

But by the grace of God I am what I am, and His grace to me was not without effect.
~ 1 Corinthians 15:10a (NIV)

Everything is a mess, scattered toys all over the yard, trash falling out of my van when I drop off the kids at school. I am ashamed. I tell myself that I could do better. As a mom and a foster parent I constantly feel thrown together. My husband and I are striving to live like Jesus, but my life is constantly being interrupted by phone calls, caseworker visits, a sick kid or last-minute work meetings. It is hard for me to let people in to see just exactly how disheveled my life truly is. My mother would be discouraged to see the state of my cluttered house.

But I raise kids who have been neglected and abused, and that is a different reality than most. I have kids who do not notice if something looks cluttered or dirty. They are only looking to see if there is food in my cupboards and I showed up to their ball game. My kids, temporary or permanent, want evidence they are secure and loved. I work hard to meet their needs, but when I lived in shame, I am filling them from an empty cup. In my embarrassment, I apologize profusely or I make excuses as to why people find our life disheveled. I keep living this chaotic life day-to-day and just hope God sees me. I make excuses in shame. I do not think I will measure up in someone else's eyes.

But God says He does not need me to measure up to someone else's standards. God says I am doing exactly what He asked me to do. God graciously fills me so I can adequately fill others with Him. I need to invite those around me in to see God at work around stacks of clothes and toys and paperwork because He is here, even in the mess. He sees through the chaos and finds me through the clutter. The God of the universe is not embarrassed by trash, laundry or exhaustion. His grace extends to me moment by moment regardless of the condition of my van, bedroom or yard. There may be dishes piled in the sink, but God's grace is in my heart.

Lord, remind me that You see me through the mess. I am Your child no matter what state my house or car or life is in. Remind me to put aside the standards that others have of my life and to accept Your grace. Thank You for pulling me out of my spiritual mess and sin to be Your child. Amen.

I am Covered by Grace

picture

Make a point today to avoid apologizing for your chaos, and live in the grace God gives.

ask

Are there standards you strive to live by that are not from God?

pray

I am Covered by Grace

Worse than My Worst Nightmare By Kimberly Krueger

But thanks be to God, who gives us the victory [making us conquerors] through our Lord Jesus Christ.
~ 1 Corinthians 15:57 (ESV)

Mothers are well acquainted with fear; I think it comes with the uterus. While raising my eleven children, I've had many fears—one was my worst nightmare. What if my kids grow up to become drug addicts or alcoholics? This wasn't some irrational conjuring, its haunting sprung from real life. Their dad struggled with drugs and alcohol, and I struggled to do damage control. Making this "what if" more daunting was this belief: If my kids end up on drugs, then I've failed as a mother. Kids on drugs is an automatic parent fail, right? I believed that, and the pressure of that false belief drove me hard. So, I was on a mission to prevent it. I worked overtime to protect my kids from finding out about their dad's addictions and from this evil world, where drugs and alcohol flow freely into precious children's hands.

In 2006, my worst nightmare came true. I learned that not only was my son doing drugs, but he'd also been caught. And since he was 17 years old, he would be tried in adult court. The reality was worse than my nightmare. The day I sat in the courtroom and watched my son be escorted in handcuffs and an orange jumpsuit ... was the lowest day of my life. I promptly put myself in my own court, too. I was charged and convicted; I failed as a mother, and it ruined my son's life forever.

Trust me when I say, "But thanks be to God, who gives us the victory [making us conquerors]" seemed like the most ironic Bible verse at that time. How in the world could God make this monumental failure into a conqueror? It was too late. After months of deep despair and crushing condemnation, the Lord spoke to me.

Did you teach your son to do drugs? "No, Lord." *Did you teach him to break the law?* "No, Lord, I taught him not to." *Did you love him the best you could with what you had?* "Yes, Lord, You know I love him so much." *He made his own choice, despite what you taught him. You did not fail as a mother. NOW there is NO condemnation in Me!* His words set me free! As the weight of that crushing condemnation lifted off me through my Lord, Jesus Christ, I took my first few steps in this life as a conqueror!

Jesus, I thank You for giving me victory and making me a conqueror over failure and condemnation! You are faithful! Amen.

I am a Conqueror

picture

Picture a time you felt like a failure - what happened to make you believe that?

ask

Can the Father see you as a failure if you are in Christ? How does the Father see you according to His Word? (Please refer to the list of Identity Scriptures in the back of this book before answer.)

pray

Vessels of Treasure By Sue Sherstad

For God, Who said, "Let brilliant light shine out of darkness," is the One Who has cascaded His light into us-the brilliant dawning light of the glorious knowledge of God as we gaze into the face of Jesus Christ. We are like common clay jars that carry this glorious treasure within so that the extraordinary overflow of power will be seen as God's, not ours. ~ 2 Corinthians 4:6-7 (TPT)

The thrill of searching for hidden and buried treasure has always excited me, so it's not surprising that one of my favorite movies is Raiders of The Lost Ark. It was a story about the search for the Ark of the Covenant, which contained the stone tablets God wrote the 10 Commandments on but also carried the Presence of God. A very precious treasure for the Hebrews to possess, for with it they conquered their enemies and were victorious! Paul tells us, "That we carry this glorious treasure in us!" The very Presence of Christ lives in us as believers by the Holy Spirit. We possess spiritual wealth beyond our imagination, the same resurrection power that raised Christ, resides in us! We are the Temple of the Holy Spirit and the treasure of His Gifts, His fruit, and His Power is buried in us.

It pleased the Father to bury this treasure in earthen vessels. Paul uses this term, "earthen vessels," to describe our weak and fragile human body, we can be easily broken like a piece of pottery. In our weakness, His strength is revealed. As we yield to the Holy Spirit, this flesh is broken daily so that the power and glory of God may be seen.

One day I was feeling inadequate, not enough. He spoke to me, "I Am enough!" He showed me the oil I have "been given" is enough. When I begin to pour the oil of the Holy Spirit out, it multiplies and becomes more than enough! He will fill the people around me in the overflow to meet their needs! I simply trust Him in obedience to His leading. I recognize that this power is not of me, but in Him alone. Beloved child, you are given His Spirit to shine forth as a bright light to those around you. The treasure of the third Person of the Godhead resides in you! Just like the Hebrews, you have victory over Satan because of His Presence and Power in you! As carriers of the glorious light of the gospel, God desires to manifest His Kingdom through us to bring healing, deliverance, and salvation. We must begin to pour out this treasure!

Heavenly Father, thank you for the treasure of the Holy Spirit. Make me a vessel of overflowing power that releases Your Kingdom to those around me. In Jesus Name! Amen.

I am a Vessel

picture

Are you willing to be used by God to pour out this treasure to others? What do you think that will look like?

ask

What did you learn of the treasure that's living inside of you?

pray

I am a Vessel

Who I'm Not By Kimberly Krueger

We are hard pressed on every side, but not crushed; perplexed, but not in despair; persecuted, but not abandoned; struck down, but not destroyed. ~ 2 Corinthians 4:8-9

Women often struggle with telling themselves what they are not. Sadly, it's the good things we're not that we most often declare to ourselves and each other. I'm not pretty. I'm not smart. I'm not the life of the party. I'm not good at this or qualified for that, and on and on. Well, God's Word has a LOT to say about who we are not ... and His list looks nothing like ours. What if we exchanged our tired, old 'not lists' for His? What if we woke up each day and declared to ourselves and our enemy all the things God's Word says we are not? Try it today!

I'm not condemned	I'm not aimless	I'm not unholy
I'm not rejected	I'm not timid	I'm not unclean
I'm not despised	I'm not empty	I'm not unworthy
I'm not unloved	I'm not bound	I'm not unequipped
I'm not unwanted	I'm not blind	I'm not forgotten
I'm not un-useful	I'm not poor	I'm not discarded
I'm not disqualified	I'm not foolish	I'm not accidental
I'm not defective	I'm not confused	I'm not misunderstood
I'm not less than	I'm not defeated	I'm not lacking
I'm not abandoned	I'm not insecure	I'm not afraid
I'm not lifeless	I'm not unsafe	
I'm not hopeless	I'm not unstable	
I'm not fruitless	I'm not unhelped	

Gracious God, thank you for all the things Your Word says I am NOT!
I trade my 'not list' in for Yours, today. Amen.

I am Not _____

picture

What does your tired, old 'not list' look like? List it here.

ask

Now, using the Scripture resource in the back of this book, find what the Word of God says about your tired, old 'not list'.

pray

I am Not

Jesus Changes Everything By Luanne Nelson

Therefore, if anyone is in Christ, the new creation has come: The old has gone, the new is here!
~ 2 Corinthians 5:17 (NIV)

It's not enough to know about Jesus, even the adversary knows about Him. When I made the decision to follow Jesus, everything changed. I came to realize my life was not my own. I had to cast off my old ways of thinking and start doing things differently in an effort to reconcile myself to Him. Everyone making that decision becomes a new creation, not merely improved, but truly transformed. Life looks – and is – completely different.

We begin to see His Creation with new eyes; we are given a heart of compassion. We don't just ignore sin, we avoid it. It's impossible to reach sinless perfection in this life; however, the redeemed Christian is being sanctified day by day, sinning less and less and truly cringing each time we miss the mark. Freed from sin, it no longer has power over us. We begin to walk in the fruit of the Spirit as described in Galatians 5:22. We learn to walk in the awesome power of the Most High God!

Jesus said to them, "Go into all the world and preach the gospel to all creation. Whoever believes and is baptized will be saved, but whoever does not believe will be condemned. And these signs will accompany those who believe: In my name they will drive out demons; they will speak in new tongues; they will pick up snakes with their hands; and when they drink deadly poison, it will not hurt them at all; they will place their hands on sick people, and they will get well." Mark 16:15-18 NIV

With my brothers and sisters in Jesus Christ, we work together toward being in constant union with Him. We study the Bible together. Ask the Holy Spirit to read it with you, too! The more we pray, the more His Holy Word begins to work in our lives. We begin to be what God intended for us all along. We become more like Him. We become aware that our "death" ends our old, sinful nature. It was buried with Him, and just as He was raised up by the Father, so are we raised up to "walk in newness of life," Romans 6:4 KJV.

That old me had to die, Lord Jesus. You knew it, I knew it. Thank You for pulling me out of the mess I made of the life You gave me. Thank You for this second chance! Please help me to stay on the right path with You. Amen.

I am Transformed

picture

Honestly, do you miss parts of your old self as God is transforming you? What are you doing about it?

ask

Are you wearing the new clothing of salvation? What do they look like? Can other people see it? Do other people want what you have? Are you showing them how to get it?

pray

Representing Him By Traci Weldie

So we are Christ's ambassadors; God is making his appeal through us. We speak for Christ when we plead, "Come back to God!" ~ 2 Corinthians 5:20 (NLT)

Traveling to Ethiopia, I was keenly aware that I was in a foreign country. As soon as a taxi driver corralled us into his cab, I knew everything about this experience was going to be different. We zigged. We zagged. We sped along streets with no street signs; everyone pretty much did whatever they wanted. A poor woman crossed the street with a load of material balanced gracefully upon her head, yet our driver still did not slow down ... at all. We missed clipping her by a hair!

As my husband and I walked down the streets of Addis, we stood head and shoulders above everyone and carried our much paler skin with a bit of embarrassment. Everywhere we went, we were pointed at, stared at, and heard people shout, 'Faranji!' It was clear we were foreigners. We traveled the year Barack Obama was elected President, so most everyone we crossed paths with would say, "Barack Obama!" and smile widely. Clearly, being an American equaled Barack Obama to them. We became acutely aware that our every action was being watched, and what we did demonstrated the nation of America to these Ethiopian citizens.

This is a picture of our lives as believers. We live in a world where God is being squeezed out. We are ambassadors, sent by God, to represent Him to a watching world. We can represent best by mimicking Jesus' actions. He visited the sick, sought out the hungry, and talked with the outcast. He chose to eat among the sinner. Too many Christians misrepresent God by being judgmental, opinionated, and downright mean toward those who disagree. Of course, Jesus did not condone sin, but He loved and served sinners. He drew them close, and then gently confronted the sin. Representing Jesus would find me full of the Fruit of the Spirit; full of love toward the homosexual; patient toward the repeat offender; joyful toward a repentant soul; kind toward someone of the opposite political affiliation; peaceful toward the alien; welcoming toward the prodigal; faithful to the adulterer; gentle toward the unbeliever; and restrained toward the irritating social media post. As Christ's Ambassadors, we must appeal to a hurting world and invite them to come to God; where all answers are found.

Dear Lord, help me remember that I represent who You are to a watching world. I pray that people would always see You through the regeneration of my life. May I be someone who exhibits the fruits of the Spirit as a faithful Ambassador of Christ. Amen.

I am an Ambassador

picture

What qualities do you think of when you think of an ambassador?

ask

How are you exhibiting the fruit of the Spirit to a watching world?

pray

I am an Ambassador

You Can't Earn It By Susan Brozek

For He made Him who knew no sin to be sin for us, that we might become the righteousness of God in Him. ~ 2 Corinthians 5:21 (NKJV)

We are the righteousness of God in Christ. How can this be when we miss the mark so often? The answer lies in Christ's finished work on the Cross. Our righteousness is our "right" standing before God, and it is not affected by what we do, it is who God says we are. This might grind uncomfortably against some teachings that state that we have to earn our righteousness. But fortunately, there is nothing we need to do to earn it; and therefore, there is nothing we can do to un-earn it, either! Our positional standing before our Lord is entirely and completely dependent upon Jesus' works at Calvary. In other words, even when we blow it, even when we think we've sinned too much to warrant God's forgiveness, the Lord says, "You are the righteousness of God in Christ."

Countless numbers of my patients have found freedom in their understanding that God's love, favor, acceptance, mercy, and grace are not dependent upon their performance. When we can truly grasp this fact and pull it into our hearts, only then we can stop beating ourselves up and punishing ourselves for being less than perfect all the time. This is not to say that we don't allow the Holy Spirit to convict us of our sins so that we genuinely repent, but it does tell us that our performance is not a causative factor in warranting this part of our identity because the keywords of 2 Corinthians 5:21 are the words "in Christ."

This side of eternity, I'm not convinced that we will ever be able to fully grasp everything that happened on that Cross where Jesus laid down His life for you and me; sometimes called 'The Great Exchange.' He became sin Who knew no sin so that we might become His righteousness. Because of Jesus' shed blood, we are viewed as righteous. Shame and condemnation cannot stand up under this powerful and life-changing truth!

Lord, I thank You that I no longer have to 'accomplish' any works on my own, or perform to earn my standing as being the righteousness of God in Christ! May I never cease to praise You for all You have done to give me a new identity in You. Amen.

I am His Righteousness

picture

The cloak of shame vs. the robe of righteousness: which one are you wearing? Describe what it looks and feels like.

ask

When you consider the fact that your identity is the righteousness of God in Christ, how does that enable you to view yourself differently?

pray

I am His Righteousness

God is a Good Father By Noreen Lessmann

I will be a Father to you, and you will be my sons and daughters, says the Lord Almighty.
~ 2 Corinthians 6:18 (NIV)

Dad carried a sad look in his eyes. The eyes are the window to the soul. He had a tough past with tragic events that left deep scars. He lost both parents at a tender age through a horrific event that he witnessed. You can not unsee what you have seen. He was raised by a loving Uncle and Aunt with four doting stepsisters. As a young adult, he endured much hardship serving in the Navy. Later, he lost the love of his life from complications days after the birth of his youngest daughter. I am that daughter.

He did the best he could. My sisters and I appreciated what he was able to give us. So much pain can have devastating effects. Dad was distant. His temper was easily enraged. My two sisters and I walked on eggshells to avoid reprieve, including physical and emotional abuse. I so longed for his attention. I wanted his approval so badly, a hug, a tender touch. I strove most of my life attempting to gain that physical, emotional and spiritual support. I searched for that support in unhealthy ways. Sadly, I never received it.

Through our identity in Christ, we are provided with a good Father as we are His sons and daughters. Our Father in Heaven fills any void that our earthly father was not able to fill. He is our source of supply and encouragement. Our powerful God knows us and cherishes us as sons and daughters. He loves us and that love knows no bounds. Do you have a gaping hole or void to fill in your heart and soul due to lack in your life? Allow God to be Abba, Papa, Daddy, your Support, your Encouragement, and Source.

Dear Father, thank You for being our support, our source of supply, our encouragement. Thank you, for adopting us as Your sons and daughters. Lead us to turn to You for support and comfort instead of turning to external, counterfeit sources that do not fill the void in our life or satisfy our deepest desire for love and acceptance.

I am Approved

picture

How does knowing that you are a child of God fill that void and change your life?

ask

Describe a time when you experienced a void to fill in your heart and soul due to lack in your life?

pray

I am Approved

Blessed By Noreen Lessmann

For you know the grace of our Lord Jesus Christ, that though He was rich, yet for your sake, He became poor, so that you through His poverty might become rich. ~ 2 Corinthians 8:9 (NIV)

Grandpa was rich beyond measure. Oh, he was not a millionaire although people would ask him, "Matt, how are you feeling?" and he would always answer, "Like a million." He was a bridge tender on the 92nd Street Bridge on the South East Side of Chicago. Grandpa was in charge of raising and lowering the bridge and maintaining it. Sometimes he was in charge of caring for me for short stints while tending to the bridge. He would allow me to ring the bell when the big ships would come through. It was thrilling to see the big ships and ring the bell. I felt so special.

Grandpa frequently said, "Well, as long as we have a roof over our head, a shirt on our backs, and food on the table ... " And then he would trail off. We all knew that to mean we were blessed and that was enough and more than enough. Grandpa was content in life. He was richly blessed in his relationship with the Lord and with the church. He had a strong sense of community and would give what he had and what he could to anyone in need.

He had a keen sense of his identity through our Lord Jesus Christ. He was indeed rich. He knew that his needs would be provided for. Indeed, our needs were met. We had a roof over our head, a shirt on our backs, and food on the table. We also had a relationship with Jesus.

Oh Lord God, we are thankful for a roof over our head, a shirt on our backs and food on the table. We are most thankful for the grace of our Lord Jesus Christ who left a glorious paradise to become lowly and relinquish all for our provision. Help us to be good stewards of all that you provide and assist us in trusting you to meet our needs. Help us tell others your story of good news, that you cherish us and provide for us. In your eyes, we are special. Amen.

I am Rich

picture

How would your level of contentment in life change if you listed the blessings and provisions God has provided for you? How can you live your life in the belief that through His poverty, you can become rich?

ask

How has God time and time again met your provisions and cared for your circumstances? How can you share this awareness with others?

pray

Run Your Race By Kimberly Krueger

However, when they measure themselves with themselves and compare themselves with one another, they are without understanding and behave unwisely. ~ 2 Corinthians 10:12b (AMPC)

When I started running, I joined a Facebook group with thousands of runners and was quickly blown away by this community! I was so moved by the way they spoke life to each other. One unforgettable post by a woman new to running announced she had just run her first mile. Struggling with her weight and its limitations made her insecure about her finishing time. While an average beginner pace is 12-15 minutes per mile, her mile took 18 minutes. Thousands of 'likes' and hundreds of comments raving about her performance and spurring her on moved me. The words "Rockstar," "Beast," and "Boss," speckled the thread, along with hundreds of fist bump, high five, and heart emojis. It was more life-giving—and dare I even say Christ-like—than anything I'd seen on Facebook, and it happened every time someone posted. Everyone was a winner, no matter how fast or slow their time.

I began to notice that when they set goals for their next race, it was never to beat other runners. The goals weren't even about coming in first, second, or third in the race. Goals were set to reach a new Personal Record (PR) or Personal Best (PB). Runners trained hard to beat their last time because they were competing with themselves. I loved this community so much, I wanted to run for the rest of my life!

Friend, If runners can do this, why can't we? We have Christ living inside of us, making us MORE able to do the things runners do! We also have a new identity, given to empower us to confidently run our race with Christ! He's mapped out a unique and glorious course for each of us, complete with our own finish lines. Comparing our race to someone else's is unwise and dangerous—we sabotage our destinies when we try running someone else's race! The only people we need ever measure ourselves against or try to be 'better than' is our former selves. So, we can spur one another on to victory! We can build each other up! We can celebrate each other's successes, because we were not created to be competition, we were created to be community. If we embrace our identity in Christ and run our own race, not only will the Kingdom advance, but we will achieve a new "Personal Best" with each passing year.

Lord, thank you for the course You've mapped out for me! I say, "Yes," to running with You! Give me the wisdom to keep my eyes on my own finish line and trust You to reach my personal best. Amen.

I am a Runner

picture

You are running the race of your life with Christ. What obstacles or distractions are getting in your way?

ask

What does God's Word say about each how to get around each obstacle or distraction you listed?

pray

I am a Runner

My Weakness, His Masterpiece By Tierney Gill

My grace is sufficient for thee: for my strength is made perfect in weakness. ~ 2 Corinthians 12:9

"Go home and live with it" (accompanied with a shrug). "You're a medical mystery, alright!" (said laughingly, as though I should laugh along). "If we find out what's wrong, we'll name it after you." (What?) I heard the above physician responses in my quest for better health and recaptured youth.

I was 17 that January evening, conducting a routine cleaning of my room when I suddenly – and inexplicably – experienced a terrible pain high up in my left shoulder and neck area. It pulsated for several torturous minutes before I staggered over to my bed and blacked out. By the time I was rushed to the doctor the following morning, my left arm was unusable. The muscles stopped working from shoulder to fingertip, the nerves continued to sporadically convulse, and the swelling around my neck was noticeably red-hot. This anomaly kicked off my next decade of identity-forming young adulthood, an identity that defined me in terms of deteriorating health; emergency rooms, numerous appointments with neurologists, general practitioners, natural health enthusiasts, and more; countless MRIs, CAT scans, diets, experimental IV therapy. I have tried – and heard – it all.

As a strong-willed go-getter, I struggled with trying to live life instead of merely survive it. I prefer to rely on myself. But when I still routinely suffer from a sporadic medical buffet of symptoms like paralysis, recurrent infections, loss of motor function and more, that is hard to do. God had, and has other plans for my identity, one based on Him and His strength instead of me and my lack thereof. 2 Corinthians 12 reminds me daily that God is transforming my physical weakness into a canvas He can paint a masterpiece upon, one that will bring Him the glory. His grace is sufficient: plainly, it is all that I need. My weakness becomes the backdrop against which His strength shines, much like the darkest backdrop of night produces the most brilliantly scintillating stars. When I literally can't stand on my own two feet, it's then I remember I'm not meant to, I am created to rely on my Savior and trust in His strength.

Heavenly Father, thank You for this Scripture which encourages me to see Your strength on display in my life, especially in my areas of weakness. Help me learn to acknowledge the sufficiency of Your grace in my daily life, equipping me to embrace who I am in You, and teaching me to glory and rely solely on Your strength and power, not my own. Amen.

I am Reliant on Him

picture

How can you embrace your weakness and infirmities going forward that the power of Christ may rest upon you?

ask

Can you think of a time in your life when your weakness allowed for Christ's strength to shine through you?

pray

I am Reliant on Him

Loss By Luanne Nelson

That is why, for Christ's sake, I delight in weaknesses, in insults, in hardships, in persecutions, in difficulties. For when I am weak, then I am strong. ~ 2 Corinthians 12:10 (NIV)

In the early 90s, I lost my beloved dad to lung cancer, my dearest friend to complications from a stroke, a brilliant mentor to old age, my sweet grandmother to suicide, and my very dear first husband who was the father of my children to death by his own hand. I suffered a miscarriage, too. In the months that followed, I lost the fight to keep my second marriage together; my lake home narrowly escaped foreclosure. I began a battle with alcohol that would last seven long and torturous years. My deep and profound grief, disguised as anger, alienated everyone around me. I ran most of my remaining friends out of my life. In retrospect, it was easier to run them out than have them die on me, too.

I was furious at God. I turned to tarot cards, sat through sessions with fortune-tellers and sought spirit mediums to contact dead loved ones. An Apache shaman healed the fingers on my left hand that were almost sliced off with a sharp knife. He assured me everything he did was through the power of "the Great One." My former husband's family shunned me for divorcing their son, obviously blaming me for his death; that loss settled deeply into my thirty-some-year-old bones. It was not until the enemy had utterly destroyed my life, with his seductively sneaky and gnarly influences that I chose to partake of, that I literally begged God for help. Begged, sobbed, surrendered. And, it was in God's perfect timing that He pulled me out of the abyss of my own despair, my tornado of anger, my hurricane of tears, the total and complete mess of my life. And, it was in that glorious moment when I heard His divine voice say to me: *"You don't have to do that anymore,"* that my life was miraculously changed in the blink of an eye.

God patiently waits for every one of us to come to Him. Hasten your heart-steps! Run to Him! No one gets through this life unscathed; He was waiting for me to come to Him the whole time. He's waiting for you, too. In our weakness, maybe even because of it, we are saved from ourselves through Him. It is in our weakness that we come to know His undeniable strength!

Thank you, merciful God Almighty, for Your healing grace. Without You, I know I truly can't do anything decently. You loved me, even in my messes. I am so grateful to You. Amen.

I am Strong in Him

picture

Do you tell others of His incredible love for us?

ask

Do you really and truthfully think you can do _____ by yourself?
Can you identify times in your life when His mercy has lifted you up?

pray

I am Strong in Him

Jesus Loves Me This I Know By Joni Jones

And because we are His children, God has sent the Spirit of His Son into our hearts, crying, "Abba! Father!" ~ Galatians 4:6 NLT

My sweet, innocent grandbabies who are smothered with unconditional love, are teaching me so much. It makes me wonder, if babies could speak would they ask ...

You are telling me that you love me. Why? You haven't known me that long. I haven't done or said anything important. I even cry, but you tell me that you love me. Why? You look at me, I look back at you and you tell me that you love me. You take care of all my needs. You hear all my cries. And you still love me. Why? You make me feel safe. You feed me. You change me. You tell me that you love me. Why? I just don't get it, but I will absorb it all. I will accept your love because that is what makes me smile. And that is what makes my eyes light up. That is what makes me look into your eyes and that is why I love you, too!

Love, unconditional love ... just because. You can't earn it or take it away. Unconditional love Just because God said so. He loves you even if you haven't known Him that long. You haven't done anything important. You haven't said anything important ... even if you cry. Unconditional Love ... Will meet all your needs. (Philippians 4:19) Hears all your cries. (Psalm 18:60) Keeps you safe. (Psalm 46) Feeds you. (Matthew 6) Changes you. (2 Corinthians 5:17) He tells you that He Loves you. Absorb it. Accept it. Because ... Jesus loves me! This I know, For the Bible tells me so; Little ones to Him belong; They are weak, but He is strong. Yes, Jesus loves me! (Anna Bartlett Warner)

That means you. Yes, you, and yes, me, because we are God's children. "And because we are His children, God has sent the Spirit of His Son into our hearts, prompting us to call out, "Abba, Father.'" (Galatians 4:6). So let's no longer just talk about it or sing about it ... instead, put on His unconditional love as our identity ... because He's put it on us!

Dear Lord, thank You that Your unconditional love has changed my identity. I am not a child of God and am forever changed because of this new identity. Help me to put on this unconditional love and live in my new name. Amen.

I am His Child

picture

What conditions do you place on yourself that block you from fully living as God's child who is smothered with unconditional love?

ask

How would you describe unconditional love?

pray

I Am Free By Michelle Meade

It was for freedom that Christ has set us free, no longer to be yoked to the bondage of slavery.
~ Galatians 5:1 (ESV)

The Children of Israel shook the sand off their sandals in contempt like slaves instead of entering The Promised Land as sons because of unresolved pain. I too was stuck in my past, living in the blame and shame of a lifetime of suffering. Failure was not for lack of trying. I devoured every book that promised love, attended every marriage conference that promised restoration, and sought every counselor that promised healing. All were frustrating and disappointing dead ends. I was looking at a process or a person instead of looking at the Promise Keeper Himself.

Layer by layer, chain by chain, God began to unpack the pain that was buried deep in my heart so that I might bring it to Him. God is the only ONE who can undo the work and effect of sin in our lives; wrongs permitted, committed and omitted by us, or against us. He longs to recalibrate us back to innocence, where all shame, blame, and pain are washed completely away by virtue of Christ's Blood. The power to free us is released through forgiveness. Forgiveness cancels our debt, cleanses our conscience, and clears the path for wholeness where we can actually walk in our Identity. The Parable in Matthew 18:23 hits this truth home; a servant was forgiven his debt of 10 million dollars, yet refused to forgive the debt of one who owed him a mere $20. The man was subsequently tortured in prison. When we refuse to pardon, unresolved pain keeps our soul bound in chains. Forgiveness is the key to freedom.

those old chains that used to bind me
they fell off now they remind me - i am free
those old feelings fear and shame
have lost their home I'm not the same - i am free
those old habits ways and deeds
no longer have a hold on me - i am free
copyright 2007 RememberMemore.com

Holy One, I fall at your feet in repentance for withholding forgiveness.
I say, Father, forgive them, they know not what they do and I freely pardon
all to step out of the chains of unresolved pain. By Your Blood.
IT IS FINISHED. Amen.

I am Free

picture

Can you imagine crying out to God in the middle of your own agony for the release of the ones who caused it? Jesus wants to enable you to forgive in that kind of pain.

ask

Why is it hardest to forgive those who have wounded you most? List every memory that still produces pain to recall, and release forgiveness today.

pray

No Regrets By Heidi Sampson

Let us not grow weary in doing good, for at the proper time we will reap a harvest ...
~ Galatians 6:9a (NIV)

Our family had the privilege of coming alongside a family in need, a brave Mama working to keep her kids safe. This experience altered what our life looked like for a time because we temporarily added kids to our family. There were moments when we thought it was wonderful and we were capable, but many other struggles we encountered led us to believe otherwise. We had been building relationships with this entire family, so, one week we invited them to church with us. It was chaotic in my mind, but there we were. All of us singing in worship.

God ordained the songs we sang that day. He knew we were in the midst of physical disorder from our children and guests, spiritual turbulence as we navigated our role in this family's life, and emotions of doubt and loneliness. All of this was happening around me as we sang: Love, fear cannot be found in You, and there will never be a day when You're uncertain of the ones You choose.

Did you catch that?! God is NEVER, NOT EVER, uncertain or doubtful of choosing ME as His own! He is sure of His calling of me as a mom, as a teacher, as His child, as a sinner, and as a caretaker of His children. How many times do I ask Him if I am truly the one He meant to call for this current task? The answer: too many times! But His Word tells me not to grow weary. God is not unsure about His decision to choose me. I must press on. I doubt Him because of how much reassurance I require. Does God know I will tire of His calling? Absolutely yes! But He would not have picked me if His purpose could not be fulfilled. His Spirit enables the ability to carry out His plans. I do not need to know what I am doing. I just need to know Him. He knows exactly what He is doing.

God, You have chosen me. Thank you for bringing me into these life circumstances right now. Help me to trust in Your choosing today. Amen.

I am Strong for the Task

picture

What have I grown weary of? Ask God for His strength to complete the task He chose for you.

ask

How would my life be different is I was confident God chose me? What steps can I make to be certain of God's call on my life?

pray

I am Strong for the Task

He Chose Me! By Sue Sherstad

"And He chose us to be His very own, joining us to Himself even before He laid the foundation of the universe! Because of his great love, he ordained us, so that we would be seen as holy in His eyes with an unstained innocence." ~ Ephesians 1:4 (TPT)

I remember as an elementary school girl I dreaded P.E. class when we were picked to be on teams. I was always one of the last chosen. I was small and not athletic, though I tried my best I never was good enough in the eyes of my classmates to be on their team. I experienced a lot of rejection in those early years, which deeply affected my confidence and self-esteem. Later, as a young woman, I came to know the Father's love and acceptance—He called me to His team!

He was thinking of you and me before He ever said, "Let there be Light!" We were in His heart as shining lights, just waiting to be released at His divinely appointed time into the earth realm. He ordained us, which means in the original Aramaic that "He marked us with His love." His Love is extravagant! He sent His Son, Jesus, before the very foundation of creation, to redeem us from sin and make us His sons and daughters. You are chosen for such a time as this with a very important assignment that He uniquely designed for you. No one else can do what He created and chose you to do. Little did I know that the Father's master plan was preparing me to be a pastor's wife. I've been ministering alongside my husband for over 26 years. At one time I never would've thought of myself to be good enough to marry a pastor. There were challenges and a lot of stretching in my soul in obeying the call of God. His Word shows us that He doesn't call the qualified, He qualifies the called. I look to Him to empower me by His Spirit.

Don't listen to the accusing words of Satan or people saying you aren't good enough. It's not your effort or works, but all that Jesus did at the cross that qualifies you. His Holy Spirit gives you the wisdom and strength you need. You are chosen, loved and restored to innocence in His eyes.

Heavenly Father, I thank you that you have chosen me as your child, You will never reject me. Show me your plan for my life and help me to fulfill it with the leading of the Holy Spirit. I praise You for Your great love which You have shown me through Your Son Jesus. I am chosen for a special purpose! Amen.

I am on Assignment

picture

How will you live differently knowing that He qualifies you for a special assignment you were chosen for?

ask

Do you see yourself chosen by God?

pray

I am on Assignment

I Am Who He Says I Am By Heather Taylor

Through our union with Christ, we too have been claimed by God as his own inheritance. Before we were even born, he gave us our destiny; that we would fulfill the plan of God who always accomplishes every purpose and plan in his heart. ~ Ephesians 1:11 (TPT)

When I started to believe God had a purpose for my life and I wasn't just here on this earth wasting space, I was set on fire. I needed to know exactly what the Bible says about who I am and what I am here for. I spent a lot of time reading, re-reading and absorbing the Word. God designed me for a purpose and I am so happy to finally be able to believe that! All the years I spent as a teenager and young adult, beating myself up with negatives about who I wasn't, and what I couldn't do, became a barrier for me. I had to go back to the Bible and retrain my brain with the truth. I had to learn who I was in God's eyes.

"God doesn't call the qualified, He qualifies the called." I have no idea who said it, but this quote changed my life. Someone said this at a retreat I was attending and although I had heard it many times before, this time it was confirmation of what God had been telling me. I knew in my heart that God was calling me to tell my story, but I couldn't figure out why. I didn't have a great story. What I did have was a burning desire to write. The desire was there all my life, but I never thought I had the talent. God saw me differently.

God says we are chosen, not forsaken; loved, not abandoned; designed specifically for our destiny, a destiny that He handcrafted. We are exactly who He made us to be and that is the only qualification we need. The rest is up to Him. He will open the doors we need to walk through. He has already provided the talent to live our purpose; we just need to see ourselves the way He sees us in order to act on it. Once I decided I am who He says I am, everything changed. I began writing, speaking and even started co-hosting a podcast. My identity in Christ is so much better than the identity I gave myself! I am called AND qualified by Him. Do you believe you are qualified in God's eyes?

Lord Jesus, Thank You for making me the one and only me and for choosing and qualifying me! I trust You to open the doors that are just for me and close the ones that are not. I am who You say I am! Amen.

I am Qualified for My Call

picture

Picture yourself fulfilling your deepest desires for God's Glory, knowing that He qualified you to fulfill them. What does that look and feel like?

ask

What is keeping you from fulfilling those desires?

pray

I am Qualified for My Call

What Washes Away My Sin? By Luanne Nelson

"In Him, we have redemption through His blood, the forgiveness of our trespasses, according to the riches of His grace, which He lavished on us. In all wisdom and insight" ~ Eph 1:7-8 (NASB)

Long ago, an insane person's hand slapped me into spiritual oblivion. I was young and naïve; he had me cornered, and he knew it. He belonged to an influential group; his position allowed him to slowly kill seeds of faith, hope, and trust. He used parts of my past against me, making things up along the way to suit his purpose. He psychologically and physically tortured me, judging and condemning me. He blackmailed me and he threatened me. He used my children as pawns against me. I was terrified. My face severely bruised, a stranger rescued us, taking us to the safety of a shelter for women and children.

Where was the redemption the nuns taught in school? I felt dirty and destroyed. What washes away the sins of our past once and for all? I finally came to know the answer: Absolutely nothing except the blood of Jesus. Either that's true or it's not. If the blood of Jesus does not wash away all of our sins completely, then we're all in a lot of trouble.

Time passed and I came to know this: He does forgive us and He does lavish His unlimited grace on us when we come to Him! Gratitude and love for Him made me loathe sin and strive to stay away from it all the more. His grace gave me permission to walk away from mean people no matter who they were or who they pretended to be. At times I cannot fathom loving myself as much as Jesus loves me. I think about my many mistakes. Then, my heart says, "If my Creator can delight in His creation of me, I suppose I need to pay attention to this." I crumple in tears, throwing my hands up in the air in total and complete resignation. That is exactly the moment when the miracle happens: He takes hold of my hands, steadies me and helps me up to walk again. Who am I to not forgive myself when my Creator has already forgiven me? Am I foolish enough to think I know better than God Himself?

Thank You, dear Father God Almighty, for sending Your beloved Son, Jesus, to save us from ourselves. Thank You for the gift of Your riches and Your grace. Thank You for tirelessly rescuing us from our own mistakes. Thank You for Your faithfulness in forgiveness! Amen.

I am Forgiven

picture

Do you look for and recognize signs of despair in any of your brothers or sisters in Christ? Do you offer to help them? Have you forgiven - truly forgiven - yourself?

ask

Is there any sin or transgression you've done that you think has not been forgiven?

pray

I am Forgiven

The Truth of Who You Are By Sue Sherstad

For I always pray to the God of our Lord Jesus Christ, the Father of glory, that He may grant you a spirit of wisdom and revelation of insight into mysteries and secrets in the deep and intimate knowledge of Him, by having the eyes of your heart flooded with light, so that you can know and understand the hope to which He has called you, and how rich is His glorious inheritance in the saints.
~ Ephesians 1:17-18 (AMP)

Our Heavenly Father is Love and the Spirit of Truth streams from His heart. He desires to pour out a new and fresh revelation of His extravagant love for His children. He created us in His image, making us His sons and daughters, calling us to sonship. The revelation of true sonship empowers us to walk in authority and dominion over the enemy to receive our glorious inheritance in Christ. God is a Good Father. He wants you to know His Love so that you will experience an intimate relationship with Him. When you know His love, you will come to know His true nature and character. You will stand steadfast with confident assurance, knowing He is faithful to His promises. As His child, you will live free from fear, depression, and condemnation. His Kingdom of righteousness, peace, and joy will manifest in your life, bringing you into alignment with His will to fulfill your calling and destiny.

Satan is a master at identity theft. He is the father of lies! He is continually crafting schemes to deceive us into living lives of spiritual poverty. Satan will have you convinced that you're not worthy of the Father's love. His voice of accusation and whispers of condemnation are sent as fiery darts fueling guilt and shame. This robs you of experiencing an intimate relationship with your loving Heavenly Father, stealing your true identity and calling of sonship. He fears that you will come to the knowledge of the truth to walk in authority and dominion, defeating him in your life!

I came to know the truth after ten years of fear resulting from a rape that happened when I was 21 years old. The revelation of the Father's love set me free from the fear of paralyzing demonic attacks I suffered at night. My confidence in His Love for me became stronger than the fear of the enemy. When I knew my true identity, an internal shift took place releasing me from prison!

Resist the lies of Satan with revelation and wisdom from God. When Paul uses the word "revelation", he is referring to something that has been veiled or hidden and suddenly becomes visible to the mind or heart. The Holy Spirit will flood your heart with light to unveil the truth of who you are. The truth is you are loved by God with a perfect love and called to sonship.

Heavenly Father, I ask for the spirit of revelation to know my calling to sonship. In Jesus Name! Amen.

I am Called to Sonship

picture

What are the lies of Satan that you can now defeat knowing you're called to sonship?

ask

What is your revelation of the Father's love and the call to sonship from these verses?

pray

I am Called to Sonship

Masterpiece By Heather Taylor

For we are God's masterpiece. He has created us anew in Christ Jesus, so we can do the good things he planned for us long ago. ~ Ephesians 2:10 (NLT)

Most of my life, I did not feel like a masterpiece. In fact, I felt much more like a three-year-old's crayon scribbles. The colors never matched and there were a lot of wavy lines going in every direction with no real beginning or end. Like that toddler's drawing, I walked through life on a path that led nowhere. I had dreams deep down, but I never seemed able to define them. The few times I thought I figured it out, I soon talked myself out of it, because reality smacked me in the face! I was quick to remind myself that I wasn't smart enough, talented enough, good enough, pretty enough, funny enough or educated enough to do whatever it was that I had been foolish enough to think I could do. The "facts" that I kept telling myself were not facts at all. They were lies. Lies that I had believed from a very young age.

When a mother receives a drawing from her three-year-old, she doesn't see scribbles and mismatched colors. She sees beauty; a one-of-a-kind priceless treasure that no one could recreate. She proudly puts the picture in a beautiful frame and displays it for all to see. We often see ourselves as that three-year old's scribbles, but we are God's masterpieces. Each one of us was designed, handcrafted in our mother's womb—made to be unique. The things we see as flaws are the exact things that cause others to relate to us.

Perhaps you can relate to how I once felt about myself? Maybe you're thinking "I'm glad she wrote this because I feel like scribbles, too." If so, there is something you should know. If I hadn't learned that I was God's masterpiece, you wouldn't be reading this because I didn't believe "scribbles" could become authors. I dropped out of high school when I was 16, and although I loved to write, I was convinced I could never be a writer. But I'm not a scribble and neither are you. You are God's masterpiece and you are so much more than the lies you believe or what you see in a mirror. God has a great plan for you, don't miss it by believing you are just a scribble mark on a piece of paper.

Lord, I ask that You open my eyes to what You see. Help me remember that I am a daughter of the highest King, that You created me in my mother's womb and have a specific plan just for me. Thank You, Father, for making me Your masterpiece. Amen.

I am His Masterpiece

picture

What would change if you saw yourself the way God sees you?

ask

Looking in the mirror, what is it about you that makes you a masterpiece?

pray

I am His Masterpiece

When I Am Weak By Susan Brozek

I pray that out of His glorious riches He may strengthen you with power through His Spirit in your inner being. ~ Ephesians 3:16 (NIV)

When you think of a strong person, what comes to mind? Is it someone who demonstrates great physical strength, such as an athlete? Is it a person who you know is going through a very challenging time of their life, yet remains quiet and composed under pressure, or one who is vocal while still fighting? All of these are legitimate examples of strength, just observable in different ways.

As an interesting contrast of how strength is often conceptualized, God's Word says, "when I am weak, then I am strong" (2 Corinthians 12:10). It seems the Lord looks at human strength in a very different way than most of us do. Ephesians 3:16 tells us that God Himself strengthens us with power through the Holy Spirit. Strength is not an attribute that we have to rely upon ourselves to obtain; it is part of who we are in Christ! In this verse, the Greek word for "strengthen" is transliterated as "krataió," which means "to be made strong in the mighty power of God." The word "power" in this verse is the Greek "dunamis", from which we get our English word "dynamite." What does this mean for us when we are desperate, exhausted, at the end of our rope and feel we can't go on any longer? We, first of all, have to acknowledge that the true source of our strength comes from the Lord, and then we need to call upon Him to strengthen us by His Spirit. This is how we walk in our identity of strength!

If you find yourself in a difficult situation that seems to have no end, my prayer is that this writing causes your hopes to be stirred. Your GOD is your strength, He is your dynamite to help you endure any situation. Your point of greatest weakness is God's point of greatest strength in and through you! Challenge yourself this day to re-evaluate how you view strength in light of what Scripture says, and what it means as a part of your identity in Christ. The "strongest" people are not necessarily those who show outward demonstrations of their strength, but those who fight to win battles we know nothing about and can do so because they are intimately acquainted with the source of their strength.

Father God, thank You for being my strength in times of greatest weakness. Thank You that because of what Jesus has done for me on Calvary, I know I can have access to Your strength through the Holy Spirit. Lord, continue to help me see my identity in You as one of strength. Help me to remember that when I feel weakest, You are strongest in me. Amen.

I am Strengthened

picture

Picture a stick of dynamite. Though relatively small, it is filled with explosive power and strength. This is a metaphorical reminder of what is available to you in Christ when you seek Him! Add your comments here.

ask

The next time you are physically or emotionally drained, will you remind yourself to call upon God so that He can provide His strength to you?

pray

I am Strengthened

I am Loved Beyond Measure By Susan Tyler

And may you have the power to understand, as all God's people should, how wide, how long, how high, and how deep his love is. ~ Ephesians 3:18 (NLT)

Every time I read this verse, I pause and let out a deep sigh. It took a very long time for me to grasp that someone could love me so immensely. I had trouble comprehending such love because I grew up feeling abandoned by my earthly father.

My parents separated when I was fourteen months old, and my mother struggled to raise my brother and me on a limited income. My childhood memories of my father were a blur. Although he lived in the same town as us, his visits were infrequent. I recall fleeting moments when I would wait for him to come and get me as he had promised, only to be disappointed time and time again. On the rare occasions that he did show up, I tried my best to be the perfect child thinking that maybe I could earn his approval and his love. At Christmas time, my mother would wrap Christmas presents for my brother and me to make us believe that they were from our father; I always knew that they were not. As a teenager, I recall writing him letters—letters full of anger and pain. I felt so unloved and wondered, "What kind of man would forsake his child?"

Thankfully, in my early 30s, my issues around abandonment dissipated when I learned that my true identity comes from my Heavenly Father. In Mark 14:36, Romans 8:15, and Galatians 4:6, Jesus and Paul refer to God as "Abba," a special term that characterized their intimate relationship with God. This realization that I was the daughter of the Highest King was empowering, so I no longer sought validation from my earthly father. God loves me so much that He was willing to sacrifice His Son for my life. His love for me is unconditional and constant. I do not have to earn His affection because His adoration for me is my birthright. And it is your birthright, too.

Dearest Abba Father, please wrap Your arms around Your dear daughter and let her feel Your never-ending adoration. Open her mind and heart so that she can receive the vastness of Your love and begin to understand how much You yearn for a tender father-daughter relationship with her. In Jesus' Name I pray, Amen.

I am Adored

picture

Like the Universe is endless, God's love for you knows no end. There is absolutely nothing that you can do that will separate you from His love. His Word says He will never leave you or forsake you. How does that change how you view your identity?

ask

Have you ever felt abandoned or rejected by someone? How does Ephesians 3:18 help you to see that situation in a different light?

pray

I am Adored

God Completes What He Begins By Marlene Dawson

For I am confident of this very thing, that He who began a good work in you will perfect it to the day of Christ Jesus. ~ Philippians 1:6 (NASB)

One of the questions I had during my first years as a Christian was, "Lord, I know you see all of my weaknesses, and I seem to fail a lot. Will You ever be able to use me?" I was well aware that I was not a very good Christian. I began smoking at thirteen, and I swore a lot. It would be years before these issues, and others were resolved. I did not get a specific answer, and it would be a while before I had a complete answer, but Philippians 1:6 is a verse that gave me hope in a "yes" answer. Thinking I had to earn my heavenly position, I thought it was my responsibility to perfect the work God started when accepted Jesus as my Savior. I began hearing excellent teachings about how spiritual growth is God's job, my job is availability. I slowly understood that it is God's job to teach, mature, and show me how to represent Christ while still being human. I thought I had to be superhuman, or phony, appearing to have no faults or flaws. There is no one who can claim those superpowers, of course.

We will always contend with our humanity while we live here on earth, something no one enjoys. We just want to be done with imperfection, already. Shouldn't we attempt perfection? Looking closely at Philippians 1:6, Paul says his confidence is in God's ability to finish the work He initiated in our life. God takes the burden to change us upon His shoulders. This should give us all a great sense of relief and even joy because we know God will do all He has promised. As believers, one of the first things we must learn is the importance of believing what God says. God did begin His work in our hearts and minds, and He always finishes what He starts. As we read the Bible, we learn that this good work God started will continue being refined until Jesus comes back to get us, or we fly away to join Him in Heaven. These truths remind us that we are forever secure in Christ because He does not look at our shortcomings, but at the Father Who informs us, "Behold, I have inscribed you on the palms of My hands ... " Isaiah 49:16 (NASB).

Dear Lord, Thank You for understanding our weaknesses and loving us completely. Amen.

I am Completed

picture

How can you live as though you are God's workmanship? How will your life look different, and how will it look the same?

ask

Read Ephesians 2:8-10 (NASB) and compare it to Philippians 1:6 (NASB).

pray

I am Completed

Where Is My Home? By Traci Weldie

But we are citizens of heaven, where the Lord Jesus Christ lives. And we are eagerly waiting for him to return as our Savior. ~ Philippians 3:20 (NLT)

My husband and I met while living in Cincinnati, OH. The day after our wedding, we moved to Columbia, SC. A few months later, we moved to Fresno, CA; shortly after that, we moved to Madera, and Modesto, CA. A transitional stint in Columbus, OH followed and then we headed further north to Milwaukee, WI. From there, Watertown, WI and now we live in South Carolina again. With each move, I tried desperately to make the current abode "home." I painted white picket fences on my daughters' bedroom walls, I displayed our favorite books in each living room, I planted flowers in colorful pots on the front porch; all in an attempt to make our family feel at home despite the new cities and states. No matter how much effort I put in, something always caused us to move again, thus we never truly settled anywhere.

I have two children born in Africa. To them, home is Ethiopia and Ghana. I have two children born in California; to them, home is the west coast. The remaining two were born in Wisconsin; to them, home is cold, long winters full of sledding and shoveling. To me, going home means driving back to Ohio, so if we ever mention "going home," there is much confusion.

The truth is we are never truly home in this life. This world is not, nor will it ever be home for us. In the Bible, followers of God are called sojourners, travelers, aliens. The only time we are described as belonging to a world is in the description of our citizenship in Heaven. But what does that even mean? My two African born children had to go through a lengthy, expensive process to become legal citizens of the US. As believers, we are called to not even consider ourselves citizens of any particular earthly country, but rather to live as citizens of Heaven. Ephesians 2:19 says, "You are no longer strangers and aliens, but you are fellow citizens with the saints and members of the household of God ... Christ Jesus himself being the cornerstone." Because of Jesus, we have been granted a new citizenship status. Because of Jesus, our home is secure. Because of Jesus, we will never need to move or find a better home or strive to paint or plant in order to feel at home.

Dear Lord, thank You for granting me citizenship of Your Kingdom. Help me to live like I am no longer a stranger, but instead a family member of God because of Christ Jesus. Amen.

I am Home in Him

picture

Where do you feel your allegiance to a "home" lies? Do you consider yourself a citizen of a country? A state? A school? How is that different from being a citizen of heaven?

ask

What would your life look like if you lived every day knowing you are already accepted in the family of God and that you don't need to do anything?

pray

I am Home in Him

Strength By Noreen Lessmann

I can do all this through Him who gives me strength. ~ *Philippians 4:13 (NIV)*

My daughter is an extraordinary coach, athlete, actress, and follower of Jesus. She wrote an interesting blog about the concept of working out—really working out to the point of exerting an optimal level of physical ability. She explained that she suffered and exerted herself willingly because extraordinary efforts yield success. However, she recently experienced an enlightening paradigm shift in her thinking illustrated by a rock climber. The rock climber casually mentioned that rock climbing utilizes the easiest possible way up a route. The rock climber focuses on easy. A new understanding was born. Physical effort and exertion may only take her so far. What may take her farther along in her pursuits is learning the easiest way, the most efficient way and a way of mindfulness. Such efficiency in movement can out-perform all the exertion, superior inbred genes, and years of athleticism training. There is joy in working out simply for the joy of working out and mastering a new skill. I like this mode of thinking. It is far less intimidating and provides hope for me in my mid-life, out of shape condition.

Oh, how my life parallels these concepts. I put in all this effort. If I just work hard enough, long enough, striving, I will obtain that all elusive success. Get the car paid, the house paid, the bills paid, the retirement paid, the Bible chapter read, the devotion read. Clean the house. Cook dinner and so it goes. My daughter reminded me of a better way—mindfulness, ease and resting in God. Jesus said my burden is light. Jesus said my yoke is easy. Jesus said I will give you rest. (Matthew 11:28-30)

The bills will get paid. The house will get cleaned. The reports will get written. What makes me so presumptuous to think I can do it in my own strength? Like rock climbing, I need to focus on easy—allowing God to reveal His plan, His timing, His will instead of my will, my plan and my timing. I can do all things through Him who gives me strength. I can do all things in mindfulness of my identity in Christ.

Oh Lord, help me to relinquish my tendency to strive. Help me to remember that there is a better way, an easier way, in relationship with You. Let me be mindful that I am able through You who gives me strength. Lord Jesus, Your burden is light and your yoke is easy. In You, I can rest. Amen.

I am Strong & Able

picture

How can you live your life differently if you live in close relationship with Jesus and in mindfulness of your identity in Christ?

ask

Where do you tend to strive in your life?

pray

I am Strong & Able

Crying Out for a Life Preserver Luanne Nelson

I have been delivered from the domain of darkness and transferred into the kingdom of His beloved Son. ~ Colossians 1:13 (ESV)

The clear blue Lucite band smoothly slid up and down the metal bar of my first abacus. It tasted just like my transistor radio when I touched my tongue to it. I played with both for hours on end, listening to scratchy songs on one while sliding groups of numbers in columns on the other. They were my favorite toys. I was seven years old. I was a good kid. Then, I answered the call of the wild. I lived the life of a chain-smoking, jet-setting bon vivant. My mom kept praying for me.

Lucite is a solid transparent plastic made of polymethyl methacrylate. The chances of you looking that up are about as slim as the chance I was going to open my Bible and look anything up back then. My late thirties brought the keen awareness I had waded into a modern batch of deadly quicksand. Sinking fast, I cried out for help. God threw me a life preserver. I grabbed it. While showering off the grit, I took a quick inventory of what I had left. Most of what wasn't lost, I ended up selling anyway.

False teachers abound today, telling us that God wants us to be rich and enjoy life to the fullest. Balderdash. Humans in the flesh respond favorably to such teachings; false teachers tell them what they want to hear. I've come to know Christ doesn't call us to become rich or accumulate stuff. Rather, He calls us to servant ministry – to give food to those who are hungry, to our homeless brothers and sisters in Him, to visit those who are sick or are in prison. He teaches us, "In everything I showed you that by working hard in this manner you must help the weak and remember the words of the Lord Jesus, that He Himself said, 'It is more blessed to give than to receive.'" Acts 20:35 NASB

Dear Jesus Lord, my Savior, and King, thank You for giving me exactly what I need today; thank You also for removing every single thing in my life You knew I didn't need. Thank You for pulling me out of the darkness and transferring me into Your Light. Thank You for that chocolate chip recipe I found the other day, too. Amen.

I am Delivered

picture

When is enough, enough? Of what? What are you doing to help others to find a way out of their dazed existence? Do you pray? Do you pray with them? Where do you look to find these lost souls?

ask

How light is your life right now? How light would you like it to be?

pray

I am Delivered

The Cross Destroyed the Power of Sin By Marlene Dawson

He canceled out every legal violation we had on our record and the old arrest warrant that stood to indict us. He erased it all - our sins, our sin-stained soul - He deleted it all, and they cannot be retrieved! Everything we once were in Adam has been placed onto His cross and nailed permanently there as a public display of cancellation. ~ Colossians 2:14 (TPT)

I wanted to be a police officer from the time I was fourteen, majoring in Law Enforcement, serving on the campus police, eventually becoming a deputy sheriff. I know about keeping the law and the consequences of breaking it. I was raised in the 1960s, a time of turmoil and cultural change in our nation's history. Television became the nightly reporter of war, watching as police and protestors clashed. Even though I eventually ended up enforcing the law, I had my share of teenage rebellion, like driving my best friend's car into a median when I was fifteen, yet choosing not to call the police or my parents. I also had an anger problem that usually went unnoticed. I remember baking a birthday cake for one of my brothers, and becoming so frustrated when he kept nibbling the frosting. When he continued, and after several warnings, I angrily threw his cake into the garbage can. I didn't care how he felt. My life was so segmented that my sensitivity was seared numb most of the time. When I was eighteen, I read The Cross and the Switchblade by David Wilkerson. This book tells about a small-town preacher going to New York to help gang members know God. It changed how I viewed God and myself. Seeing my brokenness from the viewpoint of God's unconditional love made me want to know Him, but I did not know how. A year later, my mom shared her story of God's redemptive love with me, leading me into a personal relationship with Jesus. God's love softened me. For the first time, I not only wanted to be a better person, but I believed I could become a better person.

We often see ourselves in the best light, ignoring or denying our humanity, rarely admitting our mistakes or sin. But this is not how God wants to reveal Christ to a hurting world. We get to share how we once were and how receiving God's forgiveness canceled all of our sins. When we understand the price Jesus Christ paid on His cross, His crucifixion and death purchasing our eternal lives, we will want to share our story with others. His love changed our story because Jesus canceled all our debts, erasing our sins, and deleting them forever! We can share God's wonderful salvation invitation, perhaps leading others into a personal relationship with Jesus, too.

Dear Lord, Help me to be real about my life so others can see the difference You have made. Amen.

I am Cleansed

picture

What will you tell others about what Jesus has done for you and them?

ask

What did you learn about Jesus from this verse? (Colossians 2:14 TPT)

pray

I am Cleansed

Set Your Mind By Sue Sherstad

If then, you have been raised with Christ [to a new life, thus sharing His resurrection from the dead], aim at and seek the [rich, eternal treasures] that are above, where Christ is, seated at the right hand of God. And set your minds and keep them set on what is above (the higher things), not on the things that are on the earth. ~ Colossians 3:1-2 (AMP)

If you are a child of God you have a new address. You've moved from the kingdom of darkness to the kingdom of light. You've been raised with Christ to a new heavenly position of blessing and power. Now that your spirit has been brought to life in union with Christ, there is new meaning and purpose for your life. But for the blessings of this new life to take hold, you must pursue after the eternal treasure that is yours.

Like an archer aims his arrow at his target, so you must take aim and prioritize your time in prayer, Bible study, and worship. You must make the word of God your target daily, if you aim for nothing, you'll hit it every time. As you aim at and seek the rich treasures of His kingdom, the old nature with its wrong patterns of thinking is broken off of you. By studying the word of God, His thoughts will become your thoughts causing you to live victoriously. The rich treasures of the kingdom of heaven are all the promises that Jesus died to give you. You receive them by faith as you exchange thoughts of fear for love, poverty for prosperity, sickness for health, anxiety to peace, depression to joy, condemnation to forgiven and many more.

Through this revelation, I have risen above the lies and accusations of Satan. I overcame low self-esteem and thoughts of inferiority to knowing I was chosen and loved by the Father. Our mind is the battleground where the war for our destiny and true identity in Christ is waged. Paul says in Ephesians 4:23-24, "Be constantly renewed in the spirit of your mind [having a fresh mental and spiritual attitude], and put on the new nature created in God's image in true righteousness." Continually make adjustments in your attitude to align with the word of God and His promises. Put on the new nature by walking in love, as you seek the rich eternal treasures above. As a daughter of the King, you are blessed with the riches of His kingdom. Whenever Satan attacks with fear, sickness or doubting your true identity, set your mind on Christ and receive a fresh mental and spiritual attitude.

Lord, I thank you that I am raised with you to new life. I take aim to seek You in Your Word to live the higher life.

I am Renewed in My Mind

picture

What would be an example of you taking aim to seek the rich treasures above?

ask

What is the Spirit leading you to do in obedience to this passage?

pray

I am Renewed in My Mind

Power, Love, & Self Discipline By Noreen Lessmann

For God did not give us a spirit of timidity, but a spirit of power, of love and of self-discipline.
~ 2 Timothy 1:7 (NIV)

Here, Paul reminds Timothy then, and us also now, of our true identity. In Christ, we are courageous. We have a spirit of power! This is the same power that raised Christ from the dead.

We have a spirit of love. In 1 Corinthians 13:4-8, we know love is patient; love is kind. It does not envy. It does not boast, it is not proud. It is not rude, it is not self-seeking, it is not easily angered, it keeps no record of wrongs. Love does not delight in evil but rejoices with the truth. It always protects, always trusts, always hopes, always perseveres. Love never fails. We have a spirit of self-discipline. In Christ, we have the ability to live as a conqueror. In Christ, we gain self-control over gluttony, addictions, spending, lust, and procrastination. We have the discipline to get the job done.

Do you ever tell yourself these lies? Have you ever been told these lies?

I am not very bright. How could I be so stupid? I am too weak. I am not strong.

I am not team material. I am too slow, too thin, too heavy, too tall, too short.

I am never going to get ahead. I am overwhelmed. How are things going to ever get better?
In Christ, through the Holy Spirit, we are enabled to choose truth over lies.

Remember what God has to say about it... about your identity in Christ. Remember we have a spirit of power, love, and self-discipline.

Lord God, Heavenly King, keep me mindful of who I am in Christ and whose
I am in Christ. Imprint upon my heart your image of me. Let me walk
in the spirit of courage, power, and love. Amen.

I am Disciplined

picture

Write down all the things you've learned regarding your identity in Christ, to counteract the lies you have been told.

ask

What things have you believed about yourself that are not true?

pray

God's Love Restores Our Wholeness By Marlene Dawson

For we do not have a High Priest who is unable to understand and sympathize and have a shared feeling with our weaknesses and infirmities and liability to the assaults of temptation, but One who has been tempted in every respect as we are, yet without sin. Let us then fearlessly and confidently and boldly draw near to the throne of grace (the throne of God's unmerited favor to us sinners) that we may receive mercy [for our failures] and find grace to help in good time for every need [appropriate help and well-timed help, coming just when we need it]. ~ Hebrews 4:15-16 (AMPC)

My biological dad was a World War II and Korean War veteran with horrors of war demons and a terrible temper. Today, he would be diagnosed with PTSD, but in those days he just abused me, mom, my siblings, and alcohol. He said he would kill me if I ever told, and I would be nearly thirty years old before I began telling anyone. As an adult, I was still so afraid he would come after me that I asked friends to call the police if I ever screamed: "Help!" It was easy to pretend I was alright, but the past abuse affected so much of my present, I knew I needed help. After getting counseling, and much-needed healing, I rarely spoke of the abuse, because I honestly thought no one cared. When I felt safe enough to say something, Christians would get up and leave the room, tell me to stop talking or say "get over it" because they just did not want to know. God knew all of my pain and weaknesses, and He was more than willing to lead me out of brokenness and shame. Accepting God's help made me fearless, safe, and confident enough to tell my story so others could be set free by the love of God.

Those of us who have been wounded deeply by people entrusted with loving us need to know that God cares about our brokenness and complete restoration. Those who have not been wounded in this way may not ever understand, but God does! Jesus went through all the pain and betrayals we have faced, so He could relate to our suffering and reveal the way out. Those who tried to destroy us no longer can. Weaknesses and failures no longer hold us down because Jesus shares our experiences, marking a trail out of brokenness that we can follow to wholeness. The way of Christ includes His boldness to go to our Heavenly Father for the grace, mercy, forgiveness, and healing we need to become all He planned for us. The healing process can be long when wounds are many years in the making, but God is patient and kind, and He will walk us all the way through. God is love.

Dear Lord, Thank You for your tender and unconditional love.
Thank You for never giving up on me. Amen.

I am Whole

picture

How can you live as though your healing in and through Jesus is the truth?

ask

What do you learn about Jesus from these verses?

pray

I am Whole

God Equips the Called By Noreen Lessmann

May the God of peace, who through the blood of the eternal covenant brought back from the dead our Lord Jesus, that great Shepherd of the sheep, equip you with everything good for doing his will, and may he work in us what is pleasing to him, through Jesus Christ, to whom be glory forever and ever.
~ Hebrews 13:20 (NIV)

On February 1st, late in the evening, we received a call from my son's roommates that my son was ill and was going to the hospital. My mother's intuition, aka, the Holy Spirit's leading, was initiated and I knew it was imperative that we travel to the Chicago area.

En route to the hospital, we received a call from the Emergency Room doctor that my son had a severe brain bleed. He indeed stated that my son would not survive and we needed to be prepared. It was at that moment that I heard a strong inner voice state, "This is not a drill. This is real. You have a choice. You must choose to believe. Do not pay attention to what the doctor is saying. Remember the story of Jairus (Mark 5:36) in which Jesus told the synagogue ruler, 'Don't be afraid; just believe.'" At that moment, I felt a supernatural strength, unlike anything I had ever experienced.

I told Jesus, "I believe."

Upon arriving at the hospital, things did not look good. We learned that my son had a frontal lobe mass that caused the bleeding. His brain had a midline shift. His pupils were nonreactive. And Jesus said, "Do not be afraid; just believe." Through God-ordained events, a skilled surgeon (who specialized in the surgery my son needed) was snowed in and therefore available to stabilize him and perform surgery. We were told later that our son was literally moments away from permanent brain damage or death.

The tumor was surgically removed and my son received subsequent radiation and chemotherapy as well as Rehabilitation Therapy. I am forever grateful that Jesus spared the life of my son and restored him miraculously. This event completely altered the fabric of my son and our family. We were privy to a miracle. Recovering from this ordeal required total reliance from my son on the Lord Jesus to get him through medical school step by step. God equipped him as he equips all of us to do His will. To Him be the glory.

Dear God, help us to not be afraid; only believe. Dear God, help us to trust You. You equip the called. This is our identity in Christ. Amen.

I am Equipped

picture

How will this passage enable you to move forward in your life for doing His will and His work?

ask

What is God calling you to do that is beyond your comfort zone?

pray

I am Equipped

A Best Friend By Susan Tyler

And the scripture was fulfilled that says, "Abraham believed God, and it was credited to him as righteousness," and he was called God's friend." ~ James 2:23 (NIV)

I will always remember the day I told Jesus I wanted to get to know Him intimately. I was in my early 30s and had just settled in for some quiet time. I picked up my Bible and randomly turned to 2 Thessalonians 2. This was the first time I recall seeing these Scriptures, and what I read frightened me. Verse 11 reads, "For this reason, God sends them a powerful delusion so that they will believe the lie." I repeated the word delusion—over and over again in my head. The knowledge that some people will be fooled by an imposter shook me to my core!

That evening, I boldly approached God and prayed that He would teach me to know Him intimately. I wanted a best friend type of relationship where we mutually shared our innermost desires, joys, and sorrows. We have that now—a relationship where He rejoices with me when I'm happy and He is always there to comfort me when I'm sad. A heart to heart connection. It is a rapport so strong that it will stand the test of time.

Once, long ago, I was laying in bed and I began talking to God. "Lord, you always give me hugs … do you need a hug today?" Instantly, I felt a gentle pressure and heat in my chest. I could feel God's love flood me; it was like He was touched by my question and showing me His gratitude for asking about Him! I was overwhelmed. But isn't that what friends do? Don't intimate friends know each other's touch?

When He returns, no delusion will have come upon me, because I am His friend.

Lord, I thank You that I am Your friend just as Adam was. Help me to nurture our relationship so that I can get to know You even more intimately than I do at this moment. Clear out the distractions and give me the desire to spend more time with You. Take me higher, Lord, and use me in ways that will bring You glory.
In Jesus' Name I pray, Amen.

I am His Intimate Friend

picture

Picture an intimate relationship with Jesus. What does that look like for you? What would make you feel like you and Jesus had a heart to heart connection?

ask

What may be blocking you from seeking a deeper, more intimate friendship with Jesus? Write your thoughts here.

pray

I am His Intimate Friend

Chosen By Joni Jones

But you are a chosen people, a royal priesthood, a holy nation, a people belonging to God, that you may declare the praises of Him who called out of darkness into His wonderful light. ~ I Peter 1:9

My friend has a dog named Monkey, which is a story in itself. I asked her how she chose him, and she responded, "He chose me." Out of all the puppies, he was the first puppy from the litter that greeted her. It was the first time she felt unconditional love because he chose her. With tears in my eyes, I felt her heart and thought about when I felt that same way.

To be chosen. To be loved. An overwhelming feeling when we believe that we are unconditionally loved and receive it with an open heart. Was it the moment I received my engagement ring? He chose me. Was it when my children said, "Mommy" for the first time? They chose me. Even though my husband chose me, I was constantly putting myself down. In the midst of one of my belittling sessions, my husband took it personally as he said, "I chose you." He chose me. I still cry when I think about it. Hard to believe, especially when I am not feeling or acting very lovable. In those unlovable moments, God reminds us. I chose you. Unconditional love is an undeserved love as we all have fallen short. Nonetheless... But "God demonstrates His own love for us in this: While we were still sinners, Christ died for us." (Romans 5:8 NIV)

It's a forgiving love that covers all that we have done and will do. "But I, yes I am the one who takes care of your sins—that's what I do. I don't keep a list of your sins." (Isaiah 43:25 MSG). It's an unconditional love that shouts "I love you!" "This is how God showed His love among us: He sent his one and only Son into the world that we might live through Him" (I John 4:9 NIV). Just because that is Who God is, He tells us He loves us to give us joy. "I have told you this so that My joy may be in you and that your joy may be complete " (John 15:11 NIV) Oh, the great love of the Father has lavished on us! "Greater love has no one than this: to lay down One's life for one's friends." (John 15: 13 NIV)

Because God calls us His Friends ~ and that is who we are In Him! Because He chose us!

Dear Lord, thank You for choosing me, for calling me to yourself, for loving me the way You do! I love You, too! Amen.

I am Chosen

picture

How would you live your day differently if you truly believed that you are accepted, significant and loved by God?

ask

What does being chosen mean to you?

pray

God's Love Protects Us By Marlene Dawson

See how very much our Father loves us, for he calls us his children, and that is what we are! But the people who belong to this world don't recognize that we are God's children because they don't know Him. ~ 1 John 3:1-2 (NLT)

One of the many sides of my Heavenly Father for which I am most grateful is how He has always protected me, even when I was young and naïve. When I was twelve, I saw a pony cart tied to a hitching post near a gas station. The owner came out as I was petting the pony, commenting about how his pony didn't like strangers so I must have something special. During our conversation, he invited me to his farm the following Sunday afternoon. I informed him that my dad had to work, so I couldn't go. The man offered to meet me at the gas station and bring me back, so I said I'd ask and if the answer was yes, I would be there. My mom and dad both said I could go, not even asking the man's name or where he lived. I was so excited I got there an hour early! I waited for three hours, but he never showed up. Although it broke my twelve-year-old heart, once over my heartbreak, I didn't think about it again for twenty years. I was much wiser and trusted God by then, so I asked God what had happened. He only said, "I was keeping you safe." God's loving care was enough for me.

When we have responded to God's invitation to join His family, we become His children. God is the best Father, but even His children rebel and occasionally want to handle life our own way. We have a tendency to shout, "I can do it myself!" whenever we do not want help. Adults try solving things on our own when relationships or situations falter. As children of God, though, our relationship with Him ensures we have access to Him, asking for and receiving our Father's help. God gives us the opportunity to tell others of His love when we see them struggling to do life alone. The Lord often reveals His heart in these circumstances, and He always has a reason or redemption planned even if we step beyond His boundaries. Telling others that God loves them and wants them to become His children is the best gift we can give away! God protects His own because He loves us far more than we know.

Dear Lord, Help me to remember Your lovingkindness
and faithfulness. Amen.

I am Protected

picture

How can your personal story influence someone when you tell them how much they are loved by God?

ask

Share a time when you were mocked for believing in Jesus.

pray

Fearless By Joni Jones

"There is no fear in love. But perfect love drives out fear because fear has to do with punishment. The one who fears is not made perfect in love." ~ 1 John 4:18

Fear has been my biggest enemy, as it paralyzes, stealing the joy of every blessing. Fear of failure, rejection, loneliness, and the fear of being my authentic self. If FEAR is described as False Evidence Appearing Real, then what is the false evidence that fills me so much that I am fearful of myself?

It is the lie that screams that I am not good enough to be loved perfectly when all I see are my imperfections.

It is the lie that tells me that I have to wait until I arrive before I can be loved enough, in the midst of not being enough.

It is the lie that fuels the fear of punishment because I believe I deserve to be punished.

Releasing fear's power begins with facing the "face" of fear—which is our own face since we are our fear's creator. This is only possible when we look into the Face of God—which is the Face of Love which casts out all fear. Oh, how it is that God's love is perfect in the midst of fear, enabling us to be fearlessly bold, being our true selves, unafraid of how others view us. Fearlessly believing in the One whose perfect love erases all the punishment that I believe I deserve. His perfect love is what prompts us to face our fears with courageous faith. God took this fearful one and is making me fearless as I walk clothed in His love.

Our Abba Father loves us with a perfect love that takes away the sting of punishment wrapped in fear. His love has promised us life in eternity with Him. God's perfect love is not dependent on our love for ourselves or the love of others. When someone perfectly loves you, they want the best for you. Fear makes us run away and Jesus came to bring us back because we are fearlessly loved by God. A perfect love that hates the sin but loves the sinner. Love that breaks the chain of fear and all of its' friends—anxiety, worry, and stress. Fear's power was broken on the cross and broken in my life, and I will never look at FEAR in the same way again. Now it is Forever Experiencing Abba's Redemption.

Dear Lord, I am thankful Your love for me is not dependant on anything I do, but rather is perfect because of who You are. Forgive me for letting fear creep in and listening to the lies that I am unworthy of Your love. Help me to rest in Your sacrifice knowing I am clothed forever in Your love. Amen.

I am Fearless

picture

What fear do you need to face with God's perfect love?

ask

What fear is punishing you? Or How do you punish yourself?

pray

I am Fearless

I Am An Overcomer By Susan Brozek

For everyone born of God overcomes the world. This is the victory that has overcome the world, even our faith. ~ 1 John 5:4 (NIV)

What does it mean to "overcome"? The answer is multi-faceted but a couple of examples include: a victory over adversity or when a problem no longer wields any power over us. In essence, overcomers have success in defeating something. When we are facing a battle, whether a dispute with a loved one or an addiction we can't seem to break, God tells us in His Word that we have already been deemed as overcomers! It's part of our wonderful inheritance in Christ as children of the Most High God, having been given a new parentage and bloodline upon receiving the Lord Jesus as our Savior. But the crux of the issue hinges on whether we actually believe that we are overcomers. Oftentimes, we can begin to lose hope that we'll ever be free of our problems. Then the enemy of our soul goes about doing his job: he accuses us. The devil does so with his fiery darts and railing accusations. As a result, the accusations grow and soon define you.

Along with these lies, shame sets in. And shame is by far the most difficult emotion that I help patients at my psychotherapy practice address. It's the hardest to process because shame wraps itself around identity. It says, "I am flawed or defective in some way. Something is wrong with me that I can't overcome this." Shame is even more insidious than guilt. While guilt says, "I did something wrong," shame accuses, "I am something wrong." But, God tells us that our identity is that of an overcomer, and if we cry out to Him, He will take our shame. "But the Lord God helps me; therefore I have not been disgraced; therefore I have set my face like a flint, and I know that I shall not be put to shame." Isaiah 50:7. The same power that enabled Christ to rise from the dead is within us in the form of the Holy Spirit to overcome every struggle!

Next time we find ourselves in a situation where the odds seem to be stacked against us or we are exhausted and feeling hopeless, let's remember our source. Are we trying to overcome by ourselves, or are we allowing the Lord to intervene and do for us what we cannot do on our own? Our God, who calls us overcomers, does so for a reason; He knows that when we rely on His strength, there is sure to be a lasting victory.

Lord, thank You for calling me an overcomer because You have overcome the world! I now ask that You would enable me to be victorious as I continue to run the race for Your glory. Amen.

I am an Overcomer

picture

Write about a time when an area of struggle or bondage has kept you from living your life to the fullest. Imagine how Christ could change that.

ask

Go before the Lord and ask Him to search your heart as you examine areas in your life that are challenging to overcome.

pray

I am an Overcomer

I AM Everything By Michelle Meade

I AM the Alpha and Omega, the Beginning and the End, says the Lord God, He Who is, Who was, and Who is to come, the Almighty. ~ Revelation 1:8 (NKJV)

The paradigm shift from "Try" to "Trust" is all in the knowing. You'll let little Johnny sit on Santa's lap for a photo, but if he asked to take him home you'd run! You only know a Christmas caricature, not the person. Similarly, if you only know God as the sum of ancient stories, absolute trust is unthinkable. But God's desire is for us to know Him intimately and experientially as Everything. To enable this, He will pursue us through circumstances just like every person throughout the Bible. Take Moses for example. Out of the middle of a burning bush, a Voice speaks "Hi Moses, I'm God. You are going to leave everything, return to Egypt (wanted for murder) and deliver millions of My enslaved people out of the hands of the most powerful man on earth (who happens to be your step-brother who hates your guts)." Paraphrased from Exodus 3.

Names and meanings were synonymous in Hebraic culture. So when Moses asked God "Who should I tell them that sent me?" he was really asking, "Who are You and can You be trusted?" God said, "I AM THAT I AM" (I Exist to Be)! In other words, I AM Everything you need. Because I AM a show and tell God, I will not only tell you who I AM, I will display my power before you to reveal the wonders of My person. God invites us into His story to reveal His glory. We are to know and be known in the context and constancy of His love and faithfulness, not our own. His everything consumes all failure, fear, and doubt. How beautiful to be defined by love!

'I AM Truth, I AM Love - I AM what you have need of
give me all, not just part - I will live inside your heart
every worry, every care - all your burdens I will bear
just your ashes you can bring - I'll breathe Life in everything
I AM EVERYTHING.'
Copyright 2007 RememberMEmore.com

Father God, I am so grateful Your All-Sufficiency overrides my every deficiency, making me complete in You.

I am Complete

picture

With trepidation you approach His throne, empty-handed with no worthy gifts. It is here God surprises you. He places in your hands the sum of all creation ... His heart of love.

ask

Are you willing to go to God empty-handed and simply receive? Do you Believe His Love makes you completes? Explain.

pray

I am Complete

A New Name By Kimberly Krueger

... and I will give to each a white stone, and on the stone will be engraved a new name that no one else knows except the one receiving it. ~ Revelation 2:17b (TLB)

I have called myself many names in my lifetime. Before knowing my identity in Christ, none of them were kind or uplifting. Satan had some choice names for me, too. In fact, I learned that he's the originator of every evil name and 'less than' identity ever invented. The Bible calls him 'the accuser' in Revelation 12:10, and says he accuses us (calling us names) before the Father day and night. What a wake-up call! If he's 'the accuser,' I didn't want to agree with him! This made it easier to stop calling myself names like stupid, loser, fat, dirty, etc. I began to understand that both God and Satan have an identity for me and I am free to believe either one.

Later, I was introduced to Revelation 2:17 in a book by John Eldredge. He wrote how he'd challenged his Bible Study group to take this "new name" verse literally. He told them to get alone with God and ask Him for their new name! What? You can do that!? Cool! I knew Satan's names for me, but what was God's? Both curiosity and insecurity overwhelmed me. I wondered (feared) what name God would give me. What if God didn't think much of me? Or thought I was just okay? What if my new name was, "Meh"? Curiosity won and I closed my eyes. "Lord, what new name do You give me?" I held my breath.

You are My Esther, for such a time as this. I couldn't believe my spiritual ears! How could I even be in the same hemisphere as Esther!? She was, well, Esther! At that time in my life, I couldn't even save my receipts, much less a nation of people. I couldn't fast for more than three hours, much less three days! The Lord went on, *I choose to see you as the FINISHED work I've PROMISED you'll be. I see you in the FULLNESS of your destiny, GLORIFIED by Me. Yes. You are My Esther.* I understood! My new name wasn't based on my past or my present. It reflected the future me, the finished me and hinted at my destiny. That's how He chooses your new name, too! Today, He invites you to take a sneak peek at the glorious future creature that is you... and asks that you simply believe.

Lord, I believe my new name will show me how You see me. Please give me the courage to ask You for it. Help me to choose the name you give me over every name from 'the accuser.' Amen.

I am Given a New Name

picture

Imagine Satan standing in Heaven's Courtroom accusing you before the Father. What names is he calling you? 1 John 2:1b-2 (NASB) says, "And if anyone sins, we have an Advocate with the Father, Jesus Christ the righteous; and He Himself is the propitiation for our sins..." Since Jesus Christ is our Advocate (our Attorney) in Heaven's Court, and He paid for every sin we've committed (making us INNOCENT), what do you picture the Father is saying back to Satan, your accuser?

ask

The Bible is full of stories of God giving His servants new names. Abram became Abraham, Jacob became Israel, Cephas became Peter, and Saul became Paul. Are you ready to ask God for the new name He has given you? Write what fears or questions this raises here, and then write a prayer asking for your new name below.

pray

I am Given a New Name

KNOWING AND PROFESSING **WHO YOU ARE IN CHRIST**

"You shall know the truth, and the truth shall set you free." ~ *John 8:32*

BECAUSE OF CHRIST, I AM*....

Able to do all things through Christ - Phil. 4:13

Abounding in grace - 2 Cor. 9:8

Abounding in hope - Rom. 15:4,13

Abraham's offspring - Gal. 3:29

Accepted - Rom. 15:7

Adequate - 2 Cor. 3:5

Adopted - Gal 4:5

Adversary of the devil - 1 Pet. 5:8

Alien and stranger in the world - 1 Pet. 2:11

Alive with Christ - 1 Cor 15;22

Always having all sufficiency in all things-2Cor. 9:8

Ambassador for Christ - 2 Cor. 5:20

Anointed - 1 John 2:27

Anxious for nothing - Phil. 4:6

Appointed by God - John 15:16

Assured of reward - 1 Cor. 15:58

Assured of success in Him - Prov. 16:3

Baptized into Christ - Rom. 6:3

Beautiful - Is. 61:10

Becoming a mature person - Eph. 4:13

Becoming conformed to Christ - Rom. 8:29

Belonging to God - John 17:9

Blameless at His coming - 1 Thes. 5:23

Blessed - Jer. 17:7, Eph. 1:3

Bold and confident - Eph. 2:18, 3:12

Bondservant - Ps. 116:16

Born of God - 1 John 5:18

Born again - 1 Pet. 1:23

Bought with a price - 1 Cor. 6:20

Branch, part of the True Vine - John 15:5

Bride of Christ - Is. 54:5

Brought near - Eph. 2:13

Built up - 1 Pet. 2:5

Buried with Christ through baptism - Rom. 6:4

Called - 1 Cor. 1:9

Cared for with compassion - 1 Pet. 5:7

Carried - Ex. 19:4

Child of God - John 1:12

Cherished - Eph. 5:29

Chosen - Col. 3:12

Christ is my hope - Col. 1:27

Christ is my life - Col. 3:4

Circumcised spiritually - Col. 2:11

Citizen of heaven - Phil. 3:20

Clay in the Potter's hand - Jer. 18:6

Clean - John 15:3

Cleansed - 1 John 1:7,9

Clothed with Christ - Gal. 3:27

Comforted - 2 Cor. 1:4,5

Complete in Christ - Col. 2:10

Confident - Pro. 3:26

Confident of answers to prayer - 1 John 5:14,15

Confident He'll finish me - Phil. 1:6

Confident He will never leave me - Heb. 13:5,6

Conformed to His image - Rom. 8:29

Conqueror, more than a - Rom. 8:37

Continually with God - Ps. 73:23

Controlled by the love of Christ - 2 Cor. 5:14

Created in Christ for good works - Eph. 2:10

Crucified with Him - Gal. 2:20

Dead to sin, alive to God - Rom. 6:6,11

Delighted in - Is. 42:1

Delivered - 2 Tim. 4:18

Desired - Ps. 45:11

Died and my life hidden in God - Col. 3:3

Disciple of Christ - Luke 9:23

Disciplined - Heb. 12:5-11

Drawing near with confidence - Heb. 4:16

Empowered to obey – Phil. 2:13

Encouraged – 2 Thes. 2:16,17

Enlightened – Eph. 1:18

Enriched in everything – 1 Cor. 1:5

Equipped – 2 Tim. 3:17

Eternal life – Rom. 6:23

Every good thing, having – Philemon 6

Eyes fixed on Jesus – Heb. 12:2

Favored – Ps. 5:12

Fearing God – Ps. 25:14

Fellow citizen with the saints – Eph. 2:19

Filled to the fullness of God – Col. 2:9,10

Filled with the fruit of righteousness – Phil. 1:11

Filled with the fruit of the Spirit – Gal. 5:22,23

Filled with joy – John 17:13

Filled with the knowledge of His will – Col. 1:9

Finished product in progress – Phil. 1:6

Forgiven of my sins – 1 John 1:9

Formed from the womb – Jer. 1:5

Fragrance of His knowledge – 2 Cor. 2:14,15

Free – Rom. 8:2

Freed from sin – Rom. 6:7,22

Friend of God – John 15:14,15

Fruit-bearer – John 15:5,16

Future assured – Rom. 8:18,28

Gifted – Rom. 12:6

Given all things – Rom. 8:32

Given His magnificent promises – 2 Pet. 1:3,4

Given the Holy Spirit as a pledge – 2 Cor. 1:22

God is for me – Rom. 8:31

God's gift to Christ – John 17:24

Granted grace in Christ Jesus – Rom. 5:17,20

Guarded by God – 2 Tim. 1:12

Guarded by God's peace – Phil. 4:7

Guided – Ps. 48:14

Handiwork of Christ – Eph. 2:10

Heir – Gal. 3:29, 4:7

Helped by Him – Is. 44:2

Hidden with Christ in God – Col. 3:3

His – Is. 43:1

Holy and dearly loved – Col. 3:12

Holy and blameless – Eph. 1:4

Holy – Heb. 10:10

Honored – 2 Tim. 2:21

Hope fixed – Rom. 15:4,13

Image and glory of God – 1 Cor. 11:7

In Christ Jesus – 1 Cor. 1:30

Indestructible – 1 Pet. 1:23

Indwelt by Christ Jesus – John 14:20

Indwelt by his Spirit – Rom. 8:11

Inscribed on His palms – Is. 49:16

Inseparable from His love – Rom. 8:35

Instrument of righteousness – Rom. 6:13

Joint heir with Christ – Rom. 8:17

Justified – 1 Cor. 6:11

Kept – 1 Pet. 1:5

Kingdom of priests – Rev. 1:6

Knowing all things work for good – Rom. 8:28

Knowing whom I believe – 2 Tim. 1:12

Known – 2 Tim. 2:19

Lacking no wisdom – James 1:5

Lavished with riches of His grace – Eph. 1:7,8

Laying aside the old self – Eph. 4:22-24

Led in Christ's triumph – 2 Cor. 2:14

Life abundant – 1 John 4:9, John 10:10

Life and peace in the Spirit – Rom. 8:6

Light, having – John 8:12

Light of the world – Matt. 5:14

Like a watered garden – Is. 58:11

Living Christ's life – Gal. 2:20

Living for Him – 2 Cor. 5:15

Living stone - 1 Pet. 2:5

Lord's, the - Is. 44:5
Loved constantly, unconditionally - Is. 43:4
Lover - Ps. 18:1

Made alive with Christ - Eph. 2:5
Made by Him - Ps. 100:3
Mind of Christ, having the - 1 Cor. 2:16
Member of His body - 1 Cor. 12:27
Minister of reconciliation - 2 Cor. 5:18,19
More than a conqueror - Rom. 8:37

Named - Is. 43:1
Near to God - Eph. 2:13
Needs met by his riches - Phil. 4:19
Never forsaken - Heb. 13:5
New creation - 2 Cor. 5:17
New life - Rom. 6:4
New self - Eph. 4:22-24
No condemnation - Rom. 8:1
No fear - John 14:1,27
No longer children - Eph. 4:14,15
No longer slaves to sin - Rom. 6:6
Not given a spirit of fear - 2 Tim. 1:7
Not my own - 1 Cor. 6:19
Noticed with loving concern - Ps. 33:13,14

Object of mercy - Rom. 9:23
Obtained an inheritance - Eph. 1:11
Of God's household - Eph. 2:19
On the winning side - Col. 2:15
One with Him - John 17:23,24
One spirit with Him - 1 Cor. 6:17
Overcomer - 1 John 5:4,5
Partaker of Christ - Heb. 3:14
Partaker of the divine nature - 2 Pet. 1:4
Partaker of grace - Phil. 1:7
Partaker of the promises of Christ - Eph. 3:6
Peace of God - Phil. 4:7

Peace with God - Rom. 5:1
Perfect and complete - James 1:2-4
Pilgrim and a stranger - Heb. 11:13
Possession, His special - 1 Pet. 1:18,19
Possessor of all things - 1 Cor. 3:21-23
Power/authority of God behind me - Phil. 3:21
Prayed for - Luke 22:32
Prayers go up before God - Rev. 8:4
Predestined to adoption - Eph. 1:5,11
Prepared beforehand for glory - Rom. 9:23
Presented to God holy and blameless - Col. 1:22
Pressing forward - Phil. 3:14
Priest - 1 Pet. 2:9
Protected - 2 Thes. 3:3
Provided for - Matt. 6:33
Purchased - Rev. 5:9
Purpose, having - Ps. 138:8

Qualified to share inheritance - Col. 1:12

Raised up with Christ - Eph. 2:6
Received mercy - 1 Pet. 2:10
Received the Sprit from God - 1 Cor. 2:12
Received an unshakable kingdom - Heb. 12:28
Received the riches of grace - Eph. 1:7
Reconciled to God - Rom. 5:10
Redeemed - Gal. 3:13
Refined - 1 Pet. 1:6,7
Reigning in life - Rom. 5:17
Rejoicing - Rom. 5:2,3
Renewed - 2 Cor. 4:16
Representative, His - Matt. 5:16
Rest provided - Matt. 11:28-30
Revelation from God, having - 1 Cor. 2:10,12
Rewarded by God - Is. 49:4
Rich - 2 Cor. 8:9
Righteous - Rom. 3:22,26
Righteousness of God - 2 Cor. 5:21
Rooted and built up in Him - Col. 2:7
Royalty - Rom. 5:17, 8:16,17

Royal priesthood - 1 Pet. 2:9

Safe - Ps. 4:8
Saint - Rom. 1:7
Salt of the earth - Matt. 5:13
Sanctified - 1 Thes. 5:23
Satisfied - Ps. 17:15
Saved - Eph. 2:5,8
Sealed by God with Holy Spirit - Eph. 1:13
Seated in heavenly places - Eph. 2:6
Secure - Deut. 33:12
Sent - John 20:21
Servant of Christ - Rom. 6:22
Set free - John 8:31,32,36
Sharing Christ's inheritance - Rom. 8:17
Sharing Christ's glory - John 17:22,24
Slave of righteousness - Rom. 6:18
Sheep of Christ - Ps. 23:1
Soldier - 2 Tim. 2:3,4
Son of God - Rom. 8:14
Spirit of love, power, and sound mind - 2 Tim. 1:7
Stable - Is. 33:6
Standing in His grace - Rom. 5:2
Standing firm in Christ - 2 Cor. 1:21
Steps established by the Lord - Ps. 37:23
Strengthened in Him - Eph. 3:16
Strong in the Lord - Eph. 6:10
Sustained from birth - Ps. 71:6
Sweet aroma of God - 2 Cor. 2:14,15

Temple of the living God - 1 Cor. 3:16, 6:19
Thought about - Ps. 139:17,18
Transferred to kingdom of His Son - Col. 1:13
Transformed into His image - 2 Cor. 3:18
Treasured - Deut. 14:2
Truth, walking in - John 17:7, John 4:24

Unafraid - Is. 44:2, 51:12, 16
Understood - Eph. 1:8
Understanding things given by God - 1 Cor. 2:12
United with Christ - Rom. 6:5

Upheld - Deut. 1:30,31, 33:27
Useful of His glory - Is. 43:7

Valued - Matt. 6:26, 30, 32
Victorious - 1 Cor. 15:57

Waiting for our Savior - Titus 2:13
Walking in new life - Rom. 6:4
Walking worthy of God's calling - Eph. 4:1
Washed, sanctified, justified - 1 Cor. 6:11
Wisdom, having - Col. 2:3
Witness of Christ - Acts 1:8
Worshipper of Christ - Ps. 95:6

Yielded to God - Rom. 6:13

*LIST ADAPTED FROM: Sylvia Gunter, "Prayer Portions".

Start agreeing with what God says about you today!

Amy Oaks

Amy Oaks brings combined experiences in communications and public speaking, sports business, public relations, sales, and finally as a small business owner, along with years of teaching in the health and fitness field to her current positions of Author, Writing Coach, and Editor for FEW Publications. Amy has a previously published Amazon #1 Best Seller to her credit. Amy enjoys a good walk, a good book, an occasional paddleboard excursion, and her family. She is blessed with an understanding husband, Jon; two amazing sons, Connor and Jordan; and two loving adopted dogs, Luigi and Lacy.

Eleanor Weldie

There's very little that Eleanor Weldie loves more than sipping a cup of black coffee on an early morning with her Bible opened in her lap. Eleanor is a lifelong learner of her God. She especially loves His Word - and just words in general. With a degree from Winthrop University in English, she is currently learning to channel her love for the Lord and literature into her life in the beautiful Greenville, South Carolina area. At ten years old, Eleanor proclaimed to herself, "I'm going to be an author," and she is so excited about the opportunity to have her words published and point to the truest Word--God's Word! Email Eleanor at elweldie@gmail.com.

Heather Taylor

Heather Taylor's writing career started at sixteen; today she's a two-time Amazon #1 Bestselling Author. Heather offers endless support to FEW's mission of empowering women as FEW's LEAD Ambassador. As a Keynote Speaker, she serves up raw stories and Biblical strategies with a dash of her in-your-face humor. As a FEW Certified Coach, she launches women in their relationships, businesses, and destinies. Heather's first love is her family. She loves playing with her granddaughter, laughing with her three adult children, and her thirty years of morning coffee dates with her husband, Terry. To book Heather, contact: hjtenterprise@gmail.com.

Heidi Sampson

Heidi Sampson is a Jesus loving, Midwestern girl. She has deep empathy for others and a passion for justice. God has called her and her husband to be advocates for children in foster care. Together they worked as Family Teachers at a residential group home in South Carolina where they currently reside. Through that ministry they have fostered over 60 children and adopted two active boys. Heidi loves science, Detroit sports, and her Golden Retriever Phoebe Jane. You can read more about her work with foster care and adoption at www.sampsoncircus.org.

Joni Jones

Joni Jones has the overwhelming passion to share the hope, peace, and love of the Lord, that saved her from a life long battle of poor body image and the stronghold of bulimia. She is the founder of Be Waitless Ministries, LLC, where she encourages women to live out the word of God in everyday life through speaking, daily devotional blogs, Bible teaching, and as a Certified Biblical Counselor. She is the author of the books The Breakthrough Effect & Weightless Flying Free. Joni loves being a wife, mother of three adult children, and a "Jojo" to her grandchildren, at the New Jersey shore. Visit her website at www.bewaitless.com.

Kimberly Krueger

Those closest to her say that she is "a mom to many and a friend to all." With her eyes on Jesus, Kimberly Krueger lives her highest purpose showing women their priceless value and helping them reach their God-given potential. FEW Founder, Five-time #1 Bestselling Author, Podcaster, and Keynote Speaker, Kimberly is known as a master storyteller who imparts "unbridled confidence to move forward." She is the proud mama of 7 sons and 5 daughters and says being "Noni" to her 5 beautiful grandchildren is one of life's greatest joys. Her husband, Scott, keeps her laughing, loving, and riding her Harley. Connect with Kimberly on Facebook, Instagram, or LinkedIn by searching Kimberly Joy Krueger. Learn more at: kimberlyjoykrueger.com.

Lisa Danegelis

Lisa Danegelis and her family live in the beautiful state of Wisconsin. She attended a culinary program where she fell in love with and married her instructor thirty-one years ago. Together, they own the prestigious Lee Johns™Catering. She is also a busy mom of five adopted children and a survivor of wrongly prescribed psychiatric drugs. She has a YouTube channel and Facebook group to support others on this harrowing journey. In time, she hopes to use her home as a safe haven for those in need. Lisa enjoys gardening, yoga, and writing. You may contact her at: Bakingfever@yahoo.com.

Luanne Nelson

Twenty years ago, her life changed the moment He told her, "you don't have to do that anymore." Her heart was branded forever, she belonged to Him. Today, Luanne Nelson is an ordained street minister and international motivational speaker; she is a witness, a warrior, and a wayfarer for Jesus Christ. Luanne is a #1 Best Selling Author, sharing stories of her trials and victories through the healing grace of God. A former fashion model, chain-smoker, and flaming bon vivant, Luanne was named one of the most interesting people in the city by Milwaukee Magazine, where she resides with her husband. Please visit her website at www.LuanneNelson.com.

Marlene Dawson

Marlene Dawson is a two-time #1 best-selling author. A retired Special Education paraprofessional, other jobs include executive assistant and deputy sheriff. She comes from a broken family background, raised to think the worst about herself. When she learned God loves her, and has a beautiful plan for her life, she became a born again Christian. God placed a desire in Marlene's heart to tell others about God's love for them, and the plans He has for their lives. Marlene and husband Jim live in southeast Wisconsin, and have four adult children and eight grandchildren. Visit Marlene at marlenedawson.com.

Michelle Meade

Michelle Meade is a messy masterpiece; God has turned the torn and tattered threads of her life into a woven tapestry of His Love. Michelle is an author, speaker, and the founder of Remember ME Jewelry. Her book, The Sky Is Always Blue details her divine rescue out of severe mental illness and her climb into The Father's Heart. Each poem and silver piece reflects a facet of His glory. Michelle's passion is to lead women into soaring freedom. She lives in Georgia with her husband Paul of 30 years, has 5 children, and 7 grandchildren. Follow Michelle at RememberMEmore.com.

Nilda Campuzano

Nilda Campuzano's lifelong dream has been to write and speak, but she has kept all of that to herself after believing the lie that she did not have anything good to offer the world, and that her life experiences were something to hide, not publish. Those lies came crashing down when she met women who were boldly sharing their stories and setting others free by recounting not just their falls, but their victories. Nilda is now boldly stepping out of her comfort zone and letting her breakdowns become her breakthroughs, one story at a time. Nilda resides with her three sons in Pewaukee, WI. Find her on Facebook @ Out of the Shallow and in her group for single mothers called M.a.S (Mothers and Swords.)

Noreen Lessman

Noreen's hearts desire is to simply to help others and encourage others in their walk in life. She is able to channel some of this passion in working as a therapist in a medical setting. She relies on God's wisdom and strength to be an over comer and hopes to walk along side others to also have a relationship with Christ. Noreen enjoys convincing her husband to rehabilitate homes in disrepair and dispair- leaving the home better than when we found it. She enjoys investing in real estate properties; hiking and kayaking. She loves her husband, children, family, friends, and her new rescued Springer Spaniel Gunner.

Sue Sherstad

Sue Sherstad is an ordained minister, she holds an Honorary Doctorate Degree in Humanities and has been ministering alongside her husband Dan as a team for 27 years. Sue co-authored "The Miracle Effect" and shares her testimony of "Deliverance from the Pit," her story of restoration and healing from rape. Sue's passion is to impart the Revelation of the Love of God through the teaching and preaching of the Word that sets the captive free and live victoriously for the King! Sue and her husband currently reside in Rancho Cucamonga, CA. with their daughters, Danielle and Sarah.

Susan Brozek

Susan C. Brozek, M.S.W., L.C.S.W., is Director and Founder of Healing Word Psychotherapy Services, LLC (www.healing-word.com). She has a strong call and desire to help the hurting. She has been a Licensed Clinical Christian Psychotherapist for over 20 years and has spoken at many conferences and seminars. She hosts a monthly TV broadcast called 'The Way of Healing' on the The NOW TV Network (www.thenownetwork.org), and a bi-weekly International Radio Broadcast on Blog Talk Radio. She is a #1 Bestselling Author, and her books include: 'A FEW Words on Becoming Holy, Whole and Fit', 'A FEW Words of Comfort for the Grieving', and 'HEALING WORDS: 30 Devotional Word Studies for Emotional and Spiritual Healing'. Susan and her husband Jeff live in Mequon, WI, with the frequent trip to Door County, WI.

Susan Tyler

Passionate about Jesus, Travel, Friends and Family, Susan is the founder of the Tyler Group, an organizational development firm. She holds a master's degree in Organization Development (MSOD) and is a current Ph.D. student with a concentration in Organizational Leadership. She has a wide range of expertise and regularly facilitates workshops on topics such as: change management, church administration, leadership development, team building, and diversity and inclusion. Most of all, she is passionate about helping people to discover, develop and utilize their God Given talents - for Kingdom purposes. She would love to hear from you! Contact her at susan@thetylergroup.net.

Tierney Gill

Tierney Gill is the second oldest of 17 children. Growing up homeschooled in inner-city Milwaukee, she has a wealth of stories to share of God's provision and protection in her family's lives. Her love of reading and fascination with the written word inspired her to start writing poetry and short stories at the age of 10. With this devotional, Tierney is realizing her dream of becoming a published author while also currently writing her first novel. Tierney works in state government, holds two bachelors' degrees, and will be pursuing her masters' degree. When not working, Tierney can be found with her nose buried deep in a good book, spending time with family and friends, traveling, writing, or watching her New England Patriots win another Super Bowl.

Traci Weldie

Traci Weldie lives in beautiful Greenville, SC with her husband, Joe, and their six kids. Traci is the co-founder and visionary for The Refresh Conference -Upstate, a conference for women on the foster care and adoption journey. She also is a full time Learning Specialist and loves working with high school students every day. Traci loves watching football games, taking long walks, hiking in the Blue Ridge Mountains and sitting on her back porch with her family.

Now, if anyone is enfolded into Christ, he has become an entirely new creation.
All that is related to the old order has vanished. Behold, everything is fresh and new.
2 Corinthians 5:17(TPT)

Discover your new identity through the Gospel!

I have no greater joy than to hear
that my children are walking in the truth.
3 John 4

When we walk in the truth, it brings our Father in Heaven great joy!

However, walking in the truth can only happen if we first invite the One who calls Himself "the Way, the Truth, and the Life" into our hearts. Jesus is "the Truth" and when we ask Him to be our Lord and Savior, He not only forgives us of all sin and fills our beings with His Spirit of Truth, but He makes us new!

By His work on the Cross, and the truth of His Word, we receive a new identity; we become sons and daughters. In Christ, we are washed, freed, forgiven, and adopted into His family.

Have you received your new identity in Christ? Have you asked Jesus to come into your heart and to fill you with His Spirit—the Holy Spirit—who will continually lead and guide you into all truth? If not, we invite you to do so now by praying the prayer below. Receive the free gift of salvation and your new identity today!

Father, I believe that your Son, Jesus, lived on this earth to ultimately die for me. I know I've sinned;
I've missed the mark many times and I cannot save myself.
I know that no amount of good deeds can wash me clean - but Your blood can!

Today, I choose to place my trust in the price you paid for my sins on the Cross.
I now turn from my own ways and toward You.
I want to live for you and be the person you made me to be.
Make me new. Make me like You.

I ask you to fill me with your Holy Spirit today, and to lead
and guide me into the truth about who You are and who I am, in You!
Thank You for dying for me and giving me the gift of eternal life.
Thank you for sending Your Holy Spirit to live in my heart and to guide me; today and always.

Amen.

BECOME ONE OF THE
FEW

In addition to monthly forums, women's leadership, coaching, and retreats, The Fellowship Of Extraordinary Women (FEW) is proud to stand by these impactful, engaging, and transformational books. Enjoy these titles from FEW International Publications. Most FEW books are sold on Amazon and almost all FEW authors are available to present to your church or organization.

Refer to their websites listed in the biographies of this book OR reach out to FEW International Publications Founder and President, Kimberly Joy Krueger, at www.kimberlyjoykrueger.com.

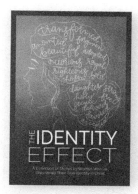
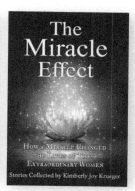

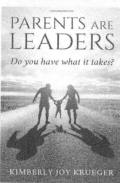

Currently seeking women authors of all levels and experience who wish to have an extraordinary experiential writing journey in a book that glorifies God.
Interested? You could be added to our list of dozens of #1 Bestselling Authors.

Contact us at thefewwomen.com.

Made in the USA
Columbia, SC
04 December 2019